MAWTS-1: 2023

ROBBIN LAIRD

CONTENTS

INTRODUCTION

In my 2013 book written with Ed Timperlake and Richard Weitz, we focused on how to rebuild American military power in the Pacific. Even though there was an announced "Pivot to the Pacific," the priority was on the land wars.

And several years of continued engagement meant that investments in systems for what later would be termed "the Great Power competition" were not made. And these land wars would be guillotined by President Biden's Blitzkrieg withdrawal from Afghanistan.

This meant that the United States had to find ways to leverage what new systems we were building and deploying to provide for coverage of the Pacific.

This would later lead to a significant shift towards oper-ating and then enhancing a distributed force. For the Air Force this was agile combat employment. For the Navy this was distributed maritime operations. For the Army it was an adventure.

The Marines are a force built to distribute and to operate with flexibility that the other services simply have not been built to do.

We argued in the book that the Marines could lead the way in Pacific force transformation, with their Osprey, with their lead role in deploying the F-35, and with the coming of their new heavy lift helicopter, the CH-53K.

And where would leadership be provided for this effort?

We argued that MAWTS-1 would have a special role, notably in working with her sister training centers. the Air Warfare Center for the USAF and NAWDC for the U.S. Navy.

We would focus on these other centers as well as the services worked to shape a new agenda and new concept of operations for a joint force able to compete with peer competitors rather than simply supporting the U.S. Army in the Middle Eastern engagements.

The role of MAWTS-1 is well laid out in a recent video produced and released by the command.[1] That video is entitled: "End of Course Video: WTI-1-24." The description of the video is as follows:

"U.S. Marines along with coalition service members, foreign and domestic, all assigned to Marine Aviation Weapons and Tactics Squadron One participated in Weapons and Tactics Instructor (WTI) course 1-24 at Marine Corps Air Station Yuma, Arizona, Sept. 10, through Oct. 29, 2023.

"WTI is an advanced, graduate-level course for selected pilots and enlisted aircrew providing standardized advanced tactical training and assists in developing and employing aviation weapons and tactics."

Another overview on MAWTS-1 was provided in an article by Sgt. Sarah Fiocco and published on April 21, 2015 as follows:

In a seven-week period, the cost of sending one Marine through Weapons and Tactics Instructors course is comparable to the cost of a four-year education at an Ivy League university.

Sponsored by Marine Aviation Weapons and Tactics Squadron 1, *the cost to graduate one certified weapons and tactics instructor from the course is $200,000. A cost, which puts each candidate through a full range of advanced aviation operations.*

The course serves to train the best pilots in the Marine Corps to return to their units as training experts. This process requires countless hours from the MAWTS-1 instructors and staff to ensure they are sending exceptionally-trained WTIs back to the fleet Marine force.

These students will be the people, who the commanding officer looks to when it comes to handling the training plan of an entire squadron," said the Academic Department Head, WTI, MAWTS-1. "He looks at them to be the guy, who says, 'We're good to go to combat.'

He's the guy the CO will trust.

Before pilots can even attend the advanced course, they must fulfill a slew of prerequisite certifications, to include low-altitude tactics instructor and air combat tactics instructor. Pilots achieve most of these certifications from their units, building their experience base in order to qualify them for the WTI course.

These pilots are already instructors before they come out here," the Academic Department Head said. "We also go see these Marines fly three to six times a year before they come to WTI.

We can say, based off our experience, if a Marine we observed is ready to go to WTI, or if they need to work on something."

On the first day of class, the pilots receive a 50-question inventory test. This is followed by nearly two months of classroom instruction, flight simulators and piloting training flights on their specific aircraft.

The course begins with instruction exclusive to each student's aircraft then expands to advance training that incorporates other platforms and units.

The students will graduate as experts on their particular aircraft, with the knowledge of how to plan and how to train others. These skills acquired from the course will ultimately be applied to their fleet units and Marine Corps operations as part of the Marine Air Ground Task Force.

During the final exercise, everyone is working together. From

close air support to battalion lifts, the whole MAGTF is involved,"
the Academic Department Head said. "When we get to that final
exercise in WTI, it's all on the students. They know how to put
together a plan and execute, so we are sitting back for the most part
just being safety backstops."

Much like the selection process for the students, the staff is selected
for the high-level of expertise they bring to course. WTI instructors'
contribution to training and standardization of coursework is what
makes WTI the valuable asset it is to the Marine Corps.

All the instructors, who teach here are handpicked," the Academic
Department Head said. "We do everything we can to ensure the fleet
is getting back the best instructors possible."

The Weapons and Tactics Instructor Course is a seven-week
course consisting of advanced tactical aviation training designed to
produce weapons and tactics instructors.

The course will serve in key training officer billets to act as a
training expert in the fleet, ensuring that Marine aviation units
continue to train effectively and to a standard across the Marine
Corps. It is courses like WTI, which reinforce the Marine Corps' role
as our nation's force in readiness.[2]

This report focuses on MAWTS-1 in 2023. In 2023, I
interviewed the CO of MAWTS-1, Col Eric Purcell, in April
and then visited the command in November after the second
WTI of the year. This provided a chance to discuss how
MAWTS-1 had progressed in working enhanced force
mobility for the USMC within the broader joint force, a key
emphasis of the force design effort.

The challenge is that while the Marines are working
FARPs and other means to enhance force mobility, the joint
force is in the throes of significant change, whether it be the
U.S. Navy working distributed maritime operations or the
USAF working agile combat employment.

How does the USMC effort to reorganize and enhance its
contribution to the joint force while the joint force is itself in

fundamental change with much uncertainty over how to do maritime distributed operations and the agile combat air combat employment?

The Navy and Air Force sides of this transition have been a major part of our work published elsewhere and provide insights with regard to how challenging the overall force transformation is within which the USMC is working to find its proper place. It is not just up to MAWTS-1 to work the training for such an effort, but NAWDC and Nellis are clearly involved as well.

To put it simply: it is a work in progress and the Marines emphasis on a MAGTF organizing principle remains important going forward in spite of the effort to find ways to operate from much smaller organizational formations.

This report includes the interviews conducted in 2023. The date indicates when the interview was published on Second Line of Defense and collectively they provide an overview of how MAWTS-1 is training for the way ahead for the USMC by preparing the force that might have to fight tonite.

As the video mentioned earlier starts: "It is not a question of if the Marine Corps will go into combat. It is only a matter of when."

I have also included an appendix that contains some additional material.

First, Ed Timperlake and I are writing a book on MAWTS-1 which we will publish next year. And in that book we have several interviews with the founders of MAWTS-1. The first commander of MAWTS wrote a piece for us which focused on that history and is included in the appendix.

Second, the F-35B has been a key element which has brought USMC and British cooperation together. But this almost did not happen and this story is the second piece.

Third, the Marines are working Osprey enabled TRAP missions as part of the maritime con-ops. The first dramatic

TRAP mission conducted by the Osprey was in Libya and we did several interviews with the Marines who did the mission. One of those interviews is included here.

---

1. https://sldinfo.com/2023/11/end-of-course-video-wti-1-24/.
2. https://www.marines.mil/News/News-Display/Article/585648/wti-sets-the-standard-for-marine-aviation/.

MAWTS-1 WORKS MOBILE BASING AND SUPPORT FOR THE DISTRIBUTED JOINT FORCE

April 26, 2023

Ever since 2018, MAWTS-1 has focused on the high-end fight component of the full spectrum of warfare. Force distribution is a key part of the survivability against a competitor who has significant firepower and can concentrate fires on relatively fixed positions.

The Marines have worked mobile basing for a long time, such as working forward refueling points and buying the Osprey and the F-35B which can operate off a wide variety of launch and landing points.

But in the past few years, the emphasis has been with regard to how to move more quickly from mobile operating bases and to do so in support of the joint force. This is a capability not only of interest to the Marines and the U.S. forces but core allies as well.

While during Laird's latest visit to Australia where there is enhanced interest, for example, in the RAAF with agile air operations, I=he spoke with the CO of MAWTS-1, Colonel Eric Purcell about how MAWTS-1 was progressing with regard to training with regard to mobile basing.

Purcell started by noting that given the close working relationship which the Marines had with the Australians, they were focused on training for such operations.

Col Purcell mentioned that last November his team met in London with U.S, and partner commands similar to MAWTS-1 in the UK. The USAF and the U.S. Navy along with Canada, and Australia discussed joint learning and training perspectives.

According to Purcell: *At the meeting last November, we looked at a number of different ways in which we can work jointly on problems such as agile combat employment, distributed maritime operations, EABOs (Expeditionary Advanced Base Operations) and F-35 integration. Canada has just recently formally joined the F-35 program, so they were not part of that discussion.*

As the Marines operate Ospreys. F-35s and now CH-53Ks, the Marines are bringing significantly capability to the evolving mobile basing function.

Mobile basing is playing a central role in the current phase of USMC transformation.

Col Purcell put it succinctly: *We are taking capability which we have had for some time, but focused on how we can move more rapidly from mobile base to mobile base. We have to find ways to make mobile bases, smaller, more distributed and persist for shorter periods of time.*

Another key aspect is that what has been a core competence of the USMC now is becoming a key capability for the wider joint and coalition force.

Col Purcell put it this way: *I think the challenge for all of the forces, whether it's the Air Force, the Army, the Navy, the Marine Corps, or the coalition forces is that the sustainment of distributed forces is challenging. How do we adapt our maintenance, logistical and sustainment systems that have been used to operating from austere bases, but now enhance the mobility of those austere bases?*

During the 2020 visits, ground artillery Marines discussed

the challenge of integrating their fires into a joint fires solution when emphasizing force distribution and mobility.

Col Purcell was asked about progress in this area. He argued that the joint fires piece is a central challenge being worked. He noted that at the recent WTI 2-23 they were working this hard. One example was incorporating the simulated integration of the future USMC Nemesis ground launch system into joint naval fires.

Part of the enhanced capability for the Marines to support force mobility was the involvement of four CH-53Ks into WTI 2-23.

Col Purcell indicated: *During the course we lifted 36K loads with the CH-53K which points to future capabilities. With regard to future capabilities, we can leverage the aircraft's ability to hold 9 to 10,000 pounds of fuel off on each of the three hooks of the CH-53K.*

The ability of each of the hooks to carry a fuel bladder is a key advantage for force mobility.

One could add that the changes in the cockpit allow for the management of such a load as well.

This is a real game changer for us at a time when we and the joint force are emphasizing distributed force logistical support and sustainability.

$\maltese$ 2 $\maltese$

THE IMPORTANCE OF INTEGRATION AND OWNERSHIP IN THE JOINT FIGHT

November 20, 2023

In my discussions with MAWTS-1 in 2020 and then my visit that year, one of the most perceptive of the officers with whom I discussed the challenges facing force integration was LtCol Barron, ADT&E Department Head at MAWTS-1.

In a 2018 interview with the then head of ADT&E, the department head described their role. According to LtCol Schiller, a key function of ADT&E is to assist in the process of informing future requirements.

It is part of our mission to help requirement officers in Headquarters Marine Corps. We do this by taking items from DARPA, research labs, industry and the PMAs and integrate them into WTI courses. We then provide an after-action report with our assessment on their performance and utility to the force.

In other words, ADT&E is focused on the core task of fighting today with the current force but also looking forward to how to enhance that force's capabilities in the near to mid-term as well.

As Barron faces the end of his career with the USMC, I

4

discussed with him what I see as a key challenge facing the U.S. forces, namely, not getting full value out of the systems which they already possess such as an F-35 global force.

I asked him how we could address this shortfall.

LtCol Barron: *I think you're absolutely right. The problem we face is how do we leverage these unique and disruptive capabilities that America and our coalition partners have, because we're not getting the full benefit of them.*

And I think the way to maximize the use of the fantastic systems that we have is by further integrating our people.

I think intelligence, command and control, and fires are the elements that need further integration. And when we think about intelligence, it is, all of our collectors, whether it is a fifth Gen aircraft that does a great job of sensing the environment, all the way down to individual threat sensors we need to be sharing that information to make a combined intelligence picture for our intelligence community, need to feed it through our command-and-control elements.

And I don't mean a single command control element, just like everything's sensing, everything is contributing to command and control architecture, and then enabling the decision makers human on the loop or in the loop, depending on the situation to enable both kinetic and non-kinetic fires.

That's very long answer.

But at the end of it, the thing that I think will enable this is ownership within each community. Ownership that this is our fight, that it's our responsibility. It's really easy to say, I'm an attack helicopter pilot, that's my job, I don't need to worry about it. It's hard to say, I'm going to support digital interoperability by passing what I see through a command-and-control architecture to someone who can make a decision.

It's also my job to win. And the way I do that is feed the common operating picture for the decision maker.

We then addressed the question of building an operational common operational picture and what that really means for a combat force.

U.S. Marine Corps Maj. Paul R. Barron, right, a UH-1Y Venom instructor assigned to Marine Aviation Weapons and Tactics Squadron One (MAWTS-1), inspects cargo to be lifted during Weapons and Tactics Instructor Course (WTI) Course 2-15 near Yuma, Ariz., April 25, 2015. U.S. Marine Corps photo by Lance Cpl. Jodson B. Graves, 2nd MAW Combat Camera/Released.

LtCol Barron: *We say we want a common operating picture. What is the reality of that? Are we going to all have a single COP? Or are we going to have multiple systems that talk together?*

There's so many different communities. Within the Marine Corps, you've got aviation command and control, you've got the ground combat element that has its own systems, you have intelligence cops, and that is just within one service.

So how do we get everybody on the same picture? Or how do we share that information? It's, a struggle. That's where in the near term, I think the rubber hits the road. What's our common message format?

He then highlighted a community within the USMC where he thinks such progress is being made.

LtCol Barron: *I think one of the ways ahead is for the communities to want that interoperability. I have found the V 22 community is really on board with their mesh network manager in the back of their aircraft. That community has embraced that airborne gateway.*

And it's phenomenal. They are medium lift pilots and crews, but if you talk to any one of our students from that community you can have a great conversation about what's going on in the back of their aircraft with respect to waveform message formats and which antenna is doing which type of transmission. It's truly remarkable.

Ownership and improved integration are cost effective force multipliers that dwarf the capability of standalone new systems.

❧ 3 ☙

THE MARINE CORPS WORKS
THE NEXT PHASE OF THEIR
USE OF UAVS

November 21, 2023

I wrote a chapter in the 2018 book entitled, *One Nation Under Drones*, which focused on the experience of the USMC with UAVs to date. I wrote this piece as the Marines were shifting from the primary focus on the land wars and to an enhanced focus on amphibious operations. During operations in Iraq and Afghanistan, the Marines joined in with the U.S. Army and used the Shadow unmanned aerial system, for similar operations as the U.S. Army was engaged in the land wars.

But concurrently with the introduction of Shadow into the Corps, the ScanEagle was also introduced. And this system would fit the trajectory of the evolution of the Corps as it moved from a primary occupation with the land wars to a "return to the sea" and the joining of unmanned systems to the significant evolution of the Amphibious-Read Group and Marine Expeditionary Unit pairing into a flexible amphibious ready task force, a change driven initially by the introduction of the Osprey but being reshaped as other manned aircraft systems come to the force and unmanned systems woven into the overall force insertion capability of the amphibious task force.

The Scan Eagle-Blackjack transition was part of the shift in focus from the land wars to amphibious at sea operations. When he wrote the essay the focus was upon shaping capabilities to be launched from a ship to support the ground maneuver element. At the time, the Marine Corps leadership was focused on a program called MUX (MAGTF Unmanned eXpeditionary UAS) which the aviation plan at the time projected initial operations in the 2025 time frame.

But as the then Deputy Commandant of Aviation, LtGen Rudder noted in 2020, that the MUX was being shelved in favor of a different approach.

I think what we discovered with the MUX program is that it's going to require a family of systems. The initial requirement had a long list of very critical requirements, but when we did the analysis and tried to fit it inside one air vehicle," they realized they had competing needs, Rudder said.

With a family of systems approach, my sense is we're going to have an air vehicle that can do some of the requirements, some of the higher-end requirements, potentially from a land-based high-endurance vehicle, but we're still going to maintain a shipboard capability, it just may not be as big as we originally configured."

The MUX program – formally the Marine Air-Ground Task Force (MAGTF) Unmanned Aerial System (UAS) Expeditionary – was meant to be a Group 5 UAS, the largest of the categories with highest altitude and greatest endurance. It would cover seven missions: command, control and communication; early warning; persistent fires; escort; electronic warfare; reconnaissance, intelligence, surveillance and target acquisition (RISTA); and tactical distribution...

Program officials realized they had a huge task ahead of them with so many separate missions, though, and early industry talks showed it may become cost-prohibitive. The seven missions were later sorted into two tiers of priority.

Still, as Rudder said, it became clear that those higher priority missions were incompatible with shipboard launch and recovery.

Power output and weight capacity, obviously you get more weight and power output with a ground-based system with a longer runway, expeditionary runway, than you can coming vertically off the back of a ship. Shipboard compatibility continues to be a challenge for all our air vehicles," Rudder said.[1]

What has happened since that time is the USMC is buying into the Reaper program and relying on a land based remotely piloted vehicle to provide the support Marines would require for their at sea and from the sea operations. The Marines leased two Reapers from General Atomics since 2018 but then moved from leasing to buying the aircraft in 2021.

When I visited MAWTS-1 in November 2023, I learned how the force was practically moving ahead. MAWTS-1 is a place focused on training an integrated USMC force, not pursing systems that are simply "fairy dust" as one Marine put it to me. It is about how to make the force ready to fight tonight and to do so more effectively.

He discussed the integration of the Reaper into USMC operations with the LtCol Edgardo Cardona, the Executive Officer at MAWTS-1, who is a former DASC officer and current MQ-9A Reaper pilot [2]

LtCol Edgardo Cardona is one of the pilots where the Marines have created a new MOS, which is the 7318 MOS.[3] The Marine Corps Reaper unlike its Predator brethren is not armed so there is not a competition between remotely piloted or manned systems in terms of being trigger pullers.

*U.S. Marines, assigned to Marine Corps Base Camp
Pendleton, and U.S. Air Force Airmen, assigned to the 432nd
Wing/432nd Air Expeditionary Wing, pose in front of an
MQ-9 Reaper at Marine Corps Base Camp Pendleton,
California, August 23, 2023. The agile combat employment
(ACE) exercise known as Agile Hunter saw an Air Force
MQ-9 remotely piloted aircraft land on Camp Pendleton, a
Marine Corps base, for the first time ever. U.S. Air Force
photo by Senior Airman Ariel O'Shea.*

It is about enhancing the relevant ISR to provide for more effective insertion of force and enabling that force in terms of their operations. This is notably one the most significant changes since Laird last came to MAWTS-1 in 2020.

The career of the XO has paralleled that of the evolution of USMC experience in UAVs so that he is both a core officer in the evolution of USMC capabilities but has also embodied the transition from the Middle East and the Marines use of Shadow, Scan Eagle, Blackjack and K-MAX. He has been on the ground floor for the introduction of the Reaper to the Marine Corps.

The XO pointed out that his earlier experience at MAWTS-1 with UAVs, the focus was on deconfliction of the UAVs designed to provide ISR for the ground combat element. Now the focus is upon integration with the air element for the overall integrated operations.

The Reaper is working with the combat air elements in

sharing a common operational picture and to enable those aircraft to have a view of the objective area prior to reaching it and to in turn to be able to enhance their ability to support the overall Marine Corps force being inserted into that objective area.

The XO underscored that MAWTS-1 was working closely with the USAF on Reaper operations and sharing experience and understanding their different operational requirements as well.

He underscored: *Our goal with Reaper operations is to create a common operational picture enabling ground force commanders or maritime component commanders to make real time decisions based on a plethora of information that we're providing. And we're also focused on fusing different data links that are coming down from different services together to create that operational picture.*

He went to note that *we see the MQ-9 as a good F-150 or a good reliable truck that can operate at long range and is reliable. But it is the payloads that are crucial to us and are ability to take the data generated by the payloads and use our digitally interoperable systems to distribute the data throughout the MAGTF.*

When he came to MAWTS-1 in 2020, he underscored:

We needed to figure out how to shape an MQ-9 program within the WTI focus of MAWTS-1. Training is a key piece in standing up a new capability and at MAWTS-1, it is about integrated MAGTF capability. We are not training a stand-alone force.

The XO noted that they reached out to the Air Force to help validate their initial MQ-9 training approach, and now they share lessons learned and share training slots when appropriate.

LtCol Cardona underscored: *We are working with the ACC and Headquarters USMC to set up an exchange program to foster the expertise required.*

Any time I have excess capacity, I will take an Air Force student and make them a WTI. And then they will return to the Air Force community. We have a Marine currently in the Air Force 26 Weapons School training program who will graduate in December.

So now we have a WTIs in the Air Force, and we're going to have USAF weapons school graduates in the Marine Corps who are Marines. And it fosters a lot of TTP development, a lot of great relationships with the Air Force.

He noted as well that they are tied in with the operational test community via VMX-1. They want to do integrated testing on new sensor suites and to be able to provide user input prior to the decision of what exactly gets produced and acquired.

Personally, I believe that the Marines will need to become major players in autonomous systems – airborne, and surface and below surface systems—but the Reaper is beginning the process. But certainly, the unique integrated mission sets the Marines work through a MAGTF will drive innovation which the joint force needs to note.

---

1. https://news.usni.org/2020/03/10/marines-ditch-mux-ship-based-drone-to-pursue-large-land-based-uas-smaller-shipboard-vehicle.
2. https://www.mca-marines.org/wp-content/uploads/0520-DASC.pdf.
3. https://www.marinecorpstimes.com/news/your-marine-corps/2020/10/12/marine-corps-creates-new-mos-for-mq-9-reaper-pilots/

❧ 4 ❧
COL PURCELL'S PERSPECTIVE ON THE IMPACT OF THE COMING OF THE CH-53K

November 22, 2023

During my visit to MAWTS-1 during the first week of November 2023, I had a chance to talk with Colonel Eric Purcell, the CO of MAWTS-1 about the coming of the CH-53K to the USMC.

This is the third new air system I have seen coming to the USMC since I have been coming to Yuma, but because it doesn't look as different as the other two did from their legacy ancestors, it is often not fully realized how important it will be for the USMC and the joint force.

Purcell is the first CH-53 pilot to be the CO of MAWTS-1 which is propitious as the CH-53K has been part of this year's WTIs at MAWTS-1. He has more than 3000 hours on the CH-53E and 130 hours on the CH-53D. He has had two deployments to Afghanistan and two to Iraq, and additional visits to both countries as well.

He noted that he wished they had not called it the CH-53 for the CH-53K is so different from the legacy aircraft. It is designed to fit into the deck space of an CH-53E and to have a reduced footprint for its maintenance as well.

14

But the big difference is associated with the broader changes across the Marine Corps. When I was last at MAWTS-1 in 2020, they were starting to work on how to enhance the deployability and mobility of the Marine Corps and to do so in formations smaller than the traditional MAGTF.

During this visit, my discussions with the department heads underscored how much work they have done in terms of doing expeditionary basing, innovations in Forward Refueling and Re-Arming points and ways to reduce the signature of the deployed force.

The CH-53K, in Col Purcell's view, contributed to that in a significant way. He focused on the ability of the King Stallion with its triple hooks to carry significant loads to operating locations without having to land and be on the ground for the time necessary to unload from the interior of the aircraft.

U.S. Marine Corps Col. Eric. D. Purcell, Marine Aviation Weapons and Tactics Squadron One (MAWTS-1) commanding officer, conducts an operations brief in support of a salvage and recovery exercise during Weapons and Tactics Instructor (WTI) course 2-23, at Auxiliary Airfield II, near Yuma, Arizona, March 17, 2023. U.S. Marine Corps photo by Lance Cpl. Ruben Padilla.

Col Purcell pointed out that the aircraft could carry significant fuel loads – 54,000 pounds of fuel -- to locations the F-35B might operate from and could do so with external lift rather than having to land.

Both the Osprey and the heavy lift helo could carry fuel inside and work as fuel providers to aircraft at a FARP. But being on the ground for significant time to do this exposed the aircraft to much greater risk than coming in and dropping off fuel from their external three hook system.

He pointed out that the legacy aircraft two hook system could lead on occasion to "uncommanded" load releases whereby the system on the aircraft would not be able to judge correctly whether loads on the hooks were compromising the safety of the aircraft. Systems on the aircraft prioritized aircraft safety over carrying loads and might jettison a load.

The CH-53K's systems can correctly determine whether

the load being carried by the aircraft affect the center of gravity of the aircraft, which is central to its security, and can make more accurate decisions with regard to the safety of the aircraft.

He noted that the load carrying capacity of the aircraft meant that it could carry an Osprey which might be in a location where it could not get repairs needed to fly safely to a location where it could be repaired. Some of the weight, such as the seats, would have to be removed to do so, but it could be done.

Col Purcell underscored that in Afghanistan and Iraq many of the missions which the CH-53E did were medium lift. The CH-53K is optimized for heavy lift and both the Marine Corps and the joint force need to focus on its unique capabilities to support distributed logistics as no other rotorcraft can do in the force. It is optimized for heavy lift, and it is important to capitalize on its unique capabilities.

The CH-53K can be part of a logistic chain involving cargo aircraft like the C-17, the C-5 and the C-130, in that it can carry 463L pallets and work with fixed wing cargo aircraft to transfer their pallets to the Super Stallion and then deliver them in places only a rotorcraft can go.

The new motors on the King Stallion allow it to operate in conditions where one would not want to operate an aging CH-53E fleet. The power margins of the new aircraft are much greater than the legacy aircraft.

Col Purcell concluded: "The force will see the impact of the revolutionary design of the CH-53K to carry heavy loads long range and to enhance significantly the logistical capability of the force and to move in and out of objective areas more rapidly than the legacy system."

5

WORKING ON THE SPECTRUM WARFARE CHALLENGE

November 27, 2023

During my visit to MAWTS-1 in 2018, the shift from operating in the land wars to dealing with challenges which could be posed by peer competitors was clearly underway. At the center of the shift was clear recognition of the need to deal with the ongoing challenge of operating in contested electro-magnetic environments.

In my meetings with PACFLEET this past April, a key aspect of the challenge facing the force is clearly spectrum warfare or signature management and deception.

My takeaway from discussions at PACFLEET was very clear. Success for distributed maritime operations requires not only assured command and control but the tissue of ISR systems enabling distributed fleet operations and adding the key element of deception through various counter-ISR systems as well.

In effect, fleet distribution built on a kill web effects infrastructure is being combined with what me be called a wake-a-mole operational capability. You can't target me, if you can't find me.

As one key Navy leader put it to me: *Counter-ISR is the number one priority for me, to deny the adversary with to high confidence in his targeting capabilities. I need to deceive them and to make a needle look like a needle in a haystack of needles. It is important to have the capability to look like a black hole in the middle of nothing.*

MAWTS-1 with its work on FARPs, force distribution, new ways to do C2 such as from systems operating out of the back of Ospreys, signature management and deception is clearly working along the same lines as PACFLEET.

I had a chance to discuss this approach with Major John Edwards, the Spectrum Warfare Department Head, when visiting MAWTS-1 in November 2023.

Edwards highlighted their work in preparing the force for the spectrum management challenges they experience and will experience within a contested electronic warfare environment. Their focus is upon ramping up the "red" threat against blue to prepare the force for the experience they have when operating in a contested environment.

They focus on showing the operational elements of the force the kind of spectrum signature they are creating when they operate to better understand the nature of spectrum warfare and how that affects their lethality and survivability in operations.

And by knowing that one can create ways to think about signature deception as well as pointed out by PACFLEET.

Edwards background is from operating in the last remaining specialized USMC airborne electronic warfare platform, the Prowler.

U.S. Marine Corps aircraft assigned to Marine Operational Test and Evaluation Squadron One takeoff from a landing zone during a Spectrum Warfare Department (SWD) training event near Yuma, Arizona, Aug. 23, 2023. SWD Marines conducted a training to intercept, identify, and locate or localize sources of intentional and unintentional radiated electromagnetic energy for the purpose of immediate threat recognition, targeting, planning and conduct of future operations. U.S. Marine Corps photo by Lance Cpl. Ruben Padilla.

The focus now is upon having the entire operational force "electronic warfare" ready, which requires consideration as well for bringing the kind of threats which red forces can be brought by an adversary to contested operations. This is always going to be a work in progress as both blue and red work the dynamically changing electronic magnetic spectrum embodied in the operating forces.

We discussed an issue as well which I have observed in both allied and U.S militaries, namely the paring down of specialized aircraft to perform the EW mission and the question of whether or not there is enough capability remaining for the specialized domain which EW or tron warfare really constitutes.

Major Edwards thought this was a valid concern and observed that the Navy currently through its Growlers provides a joint capability. He noted the USAF has officers involved with Growlers and Growlers come to MAWTS-1 as well to work with the range of capabilities which the USMC deploys.

But he felt that there needs to be a joint force commitment to expertise in this area beyond simply relying on the Growler community.

Part of the problem is simply the need to have a robust capability in this area which can inform the force with regard to training standards necessary for effective operations.

If it was felt correctly that spectrum management is now a thread running through offensive and defensive operations, where will the expertise be to inform the operational and training requirements?

❧ *6* ❧

"OUR EXCELLENCE IS A KEY
PART OF DETERRENCE"

November 27, 2023

During my November 2023 visit to MAWTS-1, I had a chance to talk with Major Kyle "Elton" McHugh, tactical air department head at MAWTS-1.

McHugh was originally a Harrier pilot who transitioned to the F-35B and served for three years with the first forward deployed F-35B squadron, VMFA-121.

The F-35 is a key part of answering the question of the how the USMC integrates with the joint force and supports the maritime fight.

The Marine Corps F-35Bs in Japan provide fifth-generation aircraft to the Marine Corps and Joint Force in the first island chain, operating off a variety of basing options, and work closely with the USAF, USN, and allied Pacific Air Forces.

U.S. Marine Corps Maj. Kyle McHugh, a pilot assigned to Marine Fighter Attack Squadron 121, currently attached to Marine Medium Tilt-Rotor Squadron 265 Reinforced, 31st Marine Expeditionary Unit (MEU), departs the flight deck of amphibious assault ship USS America (LHA 6), in the East China Sea, June 24, 2021. Photo by U.S. Marine Corps Staff Sgt. John Tetrault.

The aircraft shares common sensors, decision making systems, weapons and so on with a common U.S and allied combat fleet. In discussing the way ahead for USMC integration with the joint force, both the F-35 and the Osprey are often overlooked as key stakeholders in both current capabilities and the future force.

I asked him about his time in Japan and his perspective on working with the Japanese. He commented: "I think our enemies fear our excellence and that is a key part of deterrence.

"Working with the Japanese as they stood up their own F-35s, we shared a common mission and a common passion to defend our nations and our way of life. Our adversaries cannot ignore that commitment and the quality we bring to the fight."

Throughout our discussion, Major McHugh emphasized how the Marines have worked with the joint and coalition force on integratability of the F-35, enabling a more lethal and capable F-35 enterprise.

He noted that "there has been a concerted effort by MAWTS-1 to work with the Navy and Air Force weapon schools on F-35 integration. All the weapon school instructors meet in person twice a year. The goal is to standardize and shape a tri-service TTP manual, including Australian and British partners as well."

We also discussed the coming of the Reaper and he emphasized how its inclusion is helping to learn about and shape operations in the challenging maritime environment.

He noted that many of the students who come to WTI do not have deep knowledge of the maritime environment and Reaper data is helping in that learning process.

He noted the last Harrier class came to this year's WTI and the Hornets are soon to follow. The all F-35 Marine Corps TACAIR element will be a key part of the joint and allied integration efforts as evidenced by the work on a common training manual by the weapon school instructors.

Major McHugh concluded: "At MAWTS-1 we are focused on tactical excellence. That level of competence is critical to deterrence. The events we do at MAWTS-1, both live and simulated, are executed with distributed joint partners, empowering mission commanders to compete against the evolving threat."

❧ 7 ❧

ISR, MISSION PLANNING AND ENABLING A DISTRIBUTED FORCE

November 28, 2023

I spent parts of March and April this year in Australia and then flew to Hawaii where I visited PACFLEET and PACAF.

The Australians and the American commands are both working to build a path to enhance deterrence of China and then augment capabilities which work to reinforce that path.

Force distribution, greater allied interoperability, significant C2 and ISR capabilities enabling the distributed force to operate as a kill web with enhanced capabilities to confuse adversary targeting are the key elements for reshaping the current force.

Based on this effort, acquisition choices will either help or hinder augmentation of core capabilities to further realize this approach.

A key challenge in mission success is working effective ways for higher level commanders to work effectively with forces at the tactical edge which increasingly have ISR capabilities better than the commanders have with regard to that particular operational area.

How to proceed? As one Navy officer put it:

Higher headquarters must be able to see, understand, monitor, and adjust tactical headquarters that own battlespace and missions throughout the theater.

Higher headquarters must have the ability to see, understand and occasionally direct. But those headquarters must have borders so the tactical commanders can exercise their own creativity to deliver the fires and effects where they are operating.

The higher headquarters may have access to better information and when it does it needs to have the ability to reach out to the tactical level to tell them to do or not do something associated with the larger political and strategic picture.

He felt that they were making significant progress in commanding a distributed force, which is a core element of shaping a force capable of deterrence in the Pacific.

We are capable of commanding from various locations and can be able to see and understand how to command in the battlespace dozens of ships, hundreds of aircraft, thousands of personnel.

We are capable of seeing, understanding, and deciding what is going on in the battlespace, and tracking the enemy force using exquisite means way beyond a grease pencil and a radio call. We can and do so through links and sensor from the sea floor to the heavens.

During my visit to MAWTS-1 in November 2023, I had a chance to talk about how the intelligence aspect of working in mission command and the evolving ISR environment was being experienced by a USMC intelligence officer.

I met with Capt Liggett, a MAGTF Intelligence Officer, a U.S. Naval Academy graduate whose generation will experience very significant dynamic decades of change of both ISR and counter-ISR dynamics.

Prior to coming to MAWTS-1, her experience has been in supporting fixed wing aircraft and their mission planning. She has worked with VMFA-211 and served on the Queen Elizabeth during the Marines operating their F-35Bs from that ship.

F-35B Lightning II with Marine Fighter Attack Squadron VMFA-211 and the United Kingdom's 617 Squadron, both Carrier Strike Group 21, are secured to the flight deck aboard HMS Queen Elizabeth at sea on May 06, 2021. Credit: UK Ministry of Defence

This is a very unique experience for the British carrier was built especially to operate the F-35s and has information warfare and intelligence facilities built on the ship especially for F-35 capabilities. When I visited the ship when it was being built in Scotland, I saw those facilities being built and their functionality was explained to me at the time.

(For an analysis of how this partnership between the Brits and the Marines almost did not happen see the appendix).

Capt Liggett indicated that coming to MAWTS-1 has broadened her experience and allowed her to work the intelligence function for the mission planning of the entire air capability of the USMC, including rotorcraft and the new addition to the force, the Reaper.

I highlighted that with the kind of ISR at the tactical edge which forces have this changes the dynamic between intelligence that comes from other sources and the dialogue that goes on between operators and the intelligence function.

Capt Liggett onboard HMS Queen Elizabeth.

Capt Liggett discussed that dynamic in the following terms:

We need to communicate back and forth to ensure that we have most updated information to pass on. We are active participants in this process and working to ensure that from a collection point of view we are looking in the right locations and refining information with regard to the operational area.

The challenge is to pass data effectively to the right people at the right time and make sure we have access to resources that enables us to do that. We are also informing our pilots of what we can know and what we can't from the particular resources available to us at a particular time.

She indicated that *we are generally cueing the intelligence data and the operators at the tactical edge are then taking that with what they see in real time to prosecute targets.*

With the growing capability of ISR inherent in the force at the tactical edge – with F-35s and other local intelligence capabilities – the dialogue with the intelligence analysts and sources beyond the tactical edge with those at the tactical edge is a key part of shaping operations going forward.

❧ 8 ❧

THE GCE AND SHAPING A WAY FORWARD

November 30, 2023

During my visit to MAWTS-1 in November 2023, I had a chance to talk with Maj Scott Mahaffey, the Department Head for the Ground Combat Department.

Maj Mahaffey has been at MAWTS for three years but prior to that has had a number of deployments, including Afghanistan, with an SP-MAGTF, which involved operations in Africa, and participation in a number of exercises such as Trident Juncture in Norway in 2018, the first exercise with the Indians, in the Tiger Triumph Exercise, and exercises in the Philippines.

His background provided a very good preparation for taking on the demanding task of working the training of the GCE as it works its transition from more traditional ground operations associated with the land wars to a wider range of force insertion missions.

According to Mahaffey: *Predominantly our portion of WTI we call our Air Assault and Fires Integration course. It is a heavy flavor from a ground and ACE perspective of how to execute air assaults from battalion sized raid to a platoon-sized lift.*

The fires integration piece at least from our student's perspective is focused on fires integration with air-delivered weapons and how they can mesh and integrate with ground fires not necessarily in the close in battlespace but in the deep enclosed battlespace.

Our students are typically captains at the company level, some senior enlisted, gunnies or master sergeants, with a sprinkling of lieutenants.

They have focused on how to accomplish a company objective with close in fires, and we focus on training to give them knowledge of fires support at higher echelon support.

We are focused on training which enhances their knowledge of the broader battlespace and how F-35 or HIMARS fires provide support for a broader engagement in the battlespace.

When I was last at MAWTS in 2020, there was significant concern with deploying Marines to remote locations, even if new longer-range weapons will come on line in the next few years, with the question of fires authorities.

In the MAGTF construct, the question of who gives fires authority is clear; in the new direction to have smaller groups of Marines deployed throughout the battlespace, that question is not yet resolved.

U.S. Marine Corps Capt. Scott Mahaffey plans the day's movements with Indian Army Soldiers during exercise Tiger TRIUMPH in Kakinada, India, on Nov. 19, 2019. Tiger TRIUMPH improves U.S.-Indian partnership, readiness and interoperability. It gives the U.S. Marine Corps and Indian forces the opportunity to work together, exchange knowledge and learn from each other on a range of military operations such as humanitarian assistance disaster relief and amphibious operations. Mahaffey is the commanding officer of Easy Company, 2nd Battalion, 2nd Marine Regiment, on a Unit Deployment Program to 4th Marine Regiment, 3rd Marine Division and is a native of Orlando, Fl. (U.S. Marine Corps photo by Cpl. Jacob Hancock).

The other issue is that GCE is training in the absence of the longer-range weapons which are not yet in place. They are using data from weapons development efforts, a step up from briefing slides, to work with notional weapons, NEMESIS being a case in point.

The challenge facing the GCE is seen in this USMC 2021 description of NEMESIS.

The Navy/Marine Corps Expeditionary Ship Interdiction System successfully hit its target in support of Marine Corps Forces, Pacific, during Large Scale Exercise 21 Aug. 15, 2021. The exercise showcased the U.S. maritime forces' ability to deliver lethal, integrated all-domain naval power.

LSE 21 was a live, virtual and constructive scenario-driven, globally-integrated exercise with activities spanning 17 time zones.

LSE 21 applied and assessed developmental warfighting concepts that will define how the future Navy and Marine Corps compete, respond to crises, fight and win in conflict.

The Marine Corps' NMESIS will provide the Marine Littoral Regiment with ground based anti-ship capability to facilitate sea denial and control while persisting within the enemy's weapons engagement-zone, and LSE 21 provided a venue for the program team to validate some of those concepts.

"This scenario is representative of the real-world challenges and missions the Navy and Marine Corps will be facing together in the future," said Brig. Gen. A.J. Pasagian, commander of Marine Corps Systems Command. "This exercise also provided an opportunity for us to work alongside our service partners to refine Force Design 2030 modernization concepts."

SINKEX, the exercise scenario involving NMESIS, provided a testing environment for new and developing technologies to connect, locate, identify, target and destroy adversary threats in all domains, culminating in the live-fire demonstration of the naval strike missile against a sea-based target.

During the exercise, forward-deployed forces on expeditionary advanced bases detected and, after joint command and control collaboration with other U.S. forces, responded to a ship-based adversary.

Simultaneous impacts from multiple, dispersed weapons systems and platforms across different U.S. services—including NMESIS— engaged the threat.

NMESIS integrates established, proven sub-systems, such as the Joint Lightweight Tactical Vehicle Chassis, the Naval Strike Missile and the Fire Control System used by the Navy for NSM.

"From an acquisition perspective, NMESIS started a little over two years ago," said Joe McPherson, long range fires program manager at MCSC. "We've been able to rapidly move [on developing and fielding this system] because we're leveraging existing NSM and JLTV subsystems."

Because NMESIS is not yet a fielded capability, engineers from

MCSC managed the fire control piece of the system during the exercise. Marines, however, were able to practice maneuvering the system and validating the system's interoperability with their Naval and Air Force partners.[1]

The basic focus of the Ground Combat Department at MAWTS-1 is upon company training and awareness of higher echelon support, both actual and projected such as the case with NEMESIS.

Maj Mahaffey indicated that simulators are a key part of the training regime, which allows for lessons learned to be taken away and reflected in the simulators which are located at the Marine Corps bases as well. This allows for working the standardization aspect of the training development process.

But they don't have a simulator for a new system such as NEMESIS and are working with a notional projected system as part of their training regime. They are training in terms of working the timelines to execute a strike with the notional system to support an external fires authority.

The reality for the GCE is that currently have organic fires which allow them to operate in the close in fight. Longer range fires are in development, with HIMARS at an outer range of 300Kms being the exception.

But by and large the GCE projected in remote locations is largely capable of providing defensive capability, protecting logistical locations, or radars or items of interest, not being part of an offensive punch for the joint force.

It is a work in progress.

---

1. https://www.marcorsyscom.marines.mil/News/News-Article-Display/Article/2735502/marine-corps-successfully-demonstrates-nmesis-during-lse-21/.

❧ *9* ❧

C3 AND THE WAY AHEAD FOR THE USMC

ecember 4, 2023

C3 is the key tissue allowing for the shaping of a distributed force which can be integrated to create the desired combat effect.

During my November 2023 visit to MAWTS-1, I discussed the way ahead in this crucial area with Major Christopher Werner, the C3Department Head.

Werner is a DASC marine, as is the current XO of MAWTs.

These are Marines who focus on providing the direction for air operations supporting the ground forces, and hence are key players in shaping an integrated ground maneuver force.

Major Werner began by describing their key role, notably working with the USAF, in providing fire support for the ground forces in Afghanistan. He noted that they were able to operate within a MAGTF construct to provide significant support for the ground forces in counter-insurgency operations.

But with the shift to preparing for combat operations

against peer competitors, the focus has shifted both for the air element and the focus of C3 Marines on force integration.

The air element is now returning to air-to-air combat as well as air defense as key missions, both of which were not the focus of attention in the counter-insurgency wars.

And now the C3 effort for the USMC needs to shift from a primary focus on integration within the MAGTF to working with the joint force and using C3 to integrate relevant joint force elements to create the desired effect.

Werner noted that their cooperation with the USAF evident in Afghanistan was going forward, but there was a renewed emphasis on working with the Navy on new ways to do force integration, to which C3 needed to provide the integrating tissue.

But this was a work in progress.

Major Werner noted that officers of the same rank of his in the Navy are pushing for more effective C3 between the services, but major problems remain in terms of working with the C3 systems of the carrier task forces.

He underscored: *That is something we need to work out if we can operate as an inside force with the carrier strike groups.*

C3 for the joint force as seen with the Navy MISR officers is essentially sensor-shooter integration over a kill web.

As Major Werner put it: *What we teach in our courses is the importance of being able to take data from whatever joint or coalition forces sensors are relevant to us and blending them into data enabling shooters and fires control decision makers.*

I think that makes our community such an interesting one to work within today, notably as the joint services pursue ways to do joint command and control to create desired combat effects at the tactical edge.

U.S. Marines with Command, Control and Communication, Marine Aviation Weapons and Tactics Squadron One (MAWTS-1), board an MV-22B Osprey aircraft during an offensive air support exercise, part of Weapons and Tactics Instructor (WTI) 2-23, at Marine Corps Air Station Yuma, Arizona, April 4, 2023. U.S. Marine Corps photo by Lance Cpl. Ruben Padilla

An important focus which would enable the Marines is building on the ARG-MEU and its amphibious ships. We argued in our book on the maritime kill web how such a force could develop in the future. As we argued: *There is no area where better value could be leveraged than making dramatically better use of the amphibious fleet for extended battlespace operations.*

This requires a re-imaging of what that fleet can deliver to sea control and sea denial as well as Sea Lines of Communication (SLOC) offense and defense.

Fortunately for the sea services, such a re-imaging and reinvention is clearly possible, and future acquisitions which drive new connectors, new support elements, and enhanced connectivity could drive significant change in the value and utility of the amphibious fleet as well.

In addition, as the fleet is modernized new platform designs can be added to the force as well. And as we will address later in the book, this entails shaping variant payloads as well to be delivered from a distributed integrated amphibious fleet.

As building out the evolving fleet, larger capital ships will be supplemented and completed with a variety of smaller hull forms, both manned and autonomous, but the logistics side of enabling the fleet will grow in importance and enhance the challenges for a sustainable distributed fleet.

That is certainly why the larger capital ships – enabled by directed energy weapons as well – will see an enhanced role as mother ships to a larger lego-like cluster of smaller hull forms as well.[1]

And as maritime autonomous systems come on line, amphibious ships are well positioned for mother ship functionality in terms of launching and leveraging air and sea autonomous systems.

---

1. Robbin F, Laird, and Edward Timperlake. *A Maritime Kill Web Force in the Making: Deterrence and Warfighting in the 21st Century* (pp. 109-110). Kindle Edition.

CRAFTING A SUSTAINABLE DISTRIBUTED FORCE: MAINTENANCE AND LOGISTICS CHALLENGES

December 5, 2023

Each of the services is seeking ways to distribute their force for survivability and presence, but at the same time working through a joint lens to enhance lethality.

But the elephant in the room is sustainability, maintainability, and broader considerations of logistics support.

When visiting PACFLEET and PACAF this past April, one of the key subjects we discussed was the problem of how to have a sustainable distributed force.

How to do you support a distributed maritime force?

How do you support an Air Force doing agile combat employment?

It is no shock that when the Marines are focusing then on EABO and other approaches to force distribution that they face similar problems.

How do you maintain a force which is distributed?

One can demonstrate a FARP in which the F-35 receives fuel, but what if it needs the right kind of maintainer and the parts that are needed when it wishes to leave the FARP?

How do you move ammunition and weapons to keep a sustained moving EABO force?

Since this is not done by pixie dust, what support systems are available?

How are the personnel trained and available to do such operations?

Since the trend is away from iron mountains of weapons and material how do you create a chessboard of support for the force at the tactical edge?

To do so will require significant organizational change in DoD and the shaping of a truly joint sustainment system.

But the services are moving out on ways to distribute force in advance of any such changes.

This is obvious in a place like MAWTS-1 where the focus is upon the standardization of training for operations.

How to standardize maintenance and sustainment for the EABO focused Marines?

To be blunt this is a struggle and an effort in progress, but in my own view, the resolution of this challenge is at the joint sustainment level not simply at the USMC or U.S. Navy level.

And joint solutions can be crafted using the air systems and autonomous systems coming in the near to mid-term including USVs and UAVs.

I discussed the current situation with regard to standardization of maintenance and weapons support with three MAWTS-1 Marines. Major James J. Lay is the head of aircraft maintenance at MAWTS-1. Captain Jonathan R. Caruthers is in charge of aviation ordinance support to the aircraft operating at WTI. And Captain Tyler Thomsen who is the director of the advanced aircraft maintenance course at MAWTS-1.

U.S. Marines with Marine Heavy Helicopter Squadron 361 (HMH-361), Marine Aircraft Group 16, 3rd Marine Aircraft Wing, perform maintenance on U.S. Marine Corps CH-53E helicopters assigned to Marine Aviation Weapons and Tactics Instructor (WTI) course 1-24 at Marine Corps Air Station Yuma, Arizona, Sept. 20, 2023..Marine Corps photo by Lance Cpl. Ruben Padilla.

I had a number of take-aways from my discussion with these three very capable officers. I am not holding them responsible for how I interpreted our discussion but am crediting them with insights with regard to the whole transition challenge.

The first is simply how daunting their task really is. MAWTS-1 is not an owner of aircraft. It is a facilitator of integrated operations which means that aircraft come from the various USMC air wings, fly into Yuma and within one week, they have to make the aircraft ACE ready.

They then have to organize the maintainers as part of a command-wide training effort to shape standardization across of the force. Maintainers come from the MAWs and it is in MAWTS that best practices are brought together allowing the standardization of those practices throughout the USMC.

This obviously is ongoing learning process which is driven

by maintenance experience of the air wings in operations which then gets standardized at MAWTS-1.

U.S. Marine ordinance technicians assigned to Marine Aviation Weapons and Tactics Squadron One, prepare to load advanced precision kill weapon systems during a forward arming and refueling point exercise, part of Weapons and Tactics Instructor (WTI) course 1-24 at Landing Zone Bull Attack, near Chocolate Mountains, California, Oct. 13, 2023. U.S. Marine Corps photo by Cpl. Alejandro Fernandez.

Second, the template for provision of weapons has been the iron mountain at a base or support facility then moved out to the areas of interest.

But this template needs to be adjusted in several ways.

There needs to be a ramp up of weapons supply.

There need to be new methods and procedures to distribute weapons across a distributed force.

The work which MAWTS-1 has been doing with regard to FARPS/EABOs provide a demonstration of how challenging movement of weapons over a distributed force operational area is and the question of how to work this remains to be resolved.

The problem in part rests in acquisition. The Marines acquire ground-based ammunition: The Navy acquires weapons for the air element.

How to ensure a common adequate flow of weapons to a USMC expected to support the Navy in new ways?

Third, there is the need clearly to provide a different generation of weapons for the use of a distributed force designed to deliver integrated fires at range and distance required.

But what will be the new template to distribute such forces to an agile combat force?

In short, MAWT-1 is an incubator for testing the real world for new approaches and certainly along with the Navy and the Air Force's weapon schools will attack this challenge in real world terms.

EXPANDING THE ASSAULT SUPPORT MISSION TO A BROADER MISSION SET

December 8, 2023

During my November 2023 visit to MAWTS-1, I had a chance to meet with Maj Nicholas Peters to discuss the activities of the assault mission training part of MAWTS-1. Maj Peters is the Assault Support Department Head.

While the traditional image of assault support remains a key one – transporting Marines to a place of embarkation and ready to fight – there is growing emphasis on longer range missions and on broadening the mission set.

The Osprey and KC-130 in SP-MAGTF operated at distance. This experience is being folded into training for long range missions in the Pacific. The other members of the assault force – the rotorcraft including heavy lift – are not built for the range and speed of a combined KC-130J-Osprey mission set.

But working the broader assault package in areas of interest remains a key bread and butter capability of the USMC, and continued press of events such as the Middle East certainly reminds one of the necessities of ensuring that the Marines are range for a spectrum of operations, not just somebody's pet rock.

Earlier this year, I interviewed Col Marvel who identified a range of adaptations which the Osprey is currently going through to support the joint force.

Col Marvel underscored that expanding the mission set for the Navy's CMV-22B was certainly possible but was not in his domain of responsibility.

But the USMC is clearly expanding the payloads carried by the MV-22B which supports distributed operations, and if the three services which operate the aircraft found ways to expand their ability to cross-service each other's aircraft, they would be able to enhance such operations.

As Col Marvel put it: *The Osprey provides unique speed and range combinations with an aircraft which can land vertically. It is a very flexible aircraft which could be described as a mission-kitable aircraft.*

The Osprey has big hollow space in the rear of the aircraft that can hold a variety of mission kits dependent on the mission which you want the aircraft to support.

He emphasized that with a variety of roll-on roll-off capabilities with different payloads.

We can add the specialists in the use of a particular payload along with the payload itself to operate that payload, whether kinetic or non-kinetic, whether it is a passive or active sensor payload. We need to stop thinking about having to put the command of such payloads under the glass in the cockpit and control those payloads with a tablet.[1]

Maj Peters indicated that at MAWTS-1 they have expanded the mission sets for their Ospreys to embrace C2 and ASW efforts.

Landing on USS America was during Maj Peters time with VMM-265 and from April 2020. Credit: USMC

With regard to the C2, roll on roll of capability can provide for a variety of joint force enablement and support missions. With regard to ASW, the Osprey can deploy sonobuoys in support of the Navy's ASW mission as well, and they have exercised such capability at MAWTS-1.

A key aspect of the new emphasis for Osprey training being performed at MAWTS-1 is the TRAP mission for the Navy. Obviously, there have events in the past such as the pilot rescue in Libya which highlighted how the speed and range of the Osprey provides unique TRAP mission capabilities.

But now with the focus on Indo-PACOM and the concern for loss of aircraft in a contested operation, it is important for the U.S. Navy to rely on the speed and range of the Osprey to support the TRAP mission.

Here the Osprey community is working hoisting methods

to provide for the mission, and this has become part of the training conducted by the Assault Support Department.

The Osprey is flown by the USAF and Navy as well, which leads to a kind of built in joint integration in terms of a common operator pool across the services.

Peters indicated that a USAF Osprey pilot was an instructor in his department and taught the students how the USAF using its Ospreys and operated them differently from the USMC.

And my visits to North Island with the CMV-22B squadrons certainly underscores that with the Navy operating their version of the Osprey, there are significant opportunities for working maritime integration at a very fundamental support and assault level as well.

---

1. https://sldinfo.com/2023/02/a-mission-kitable-aircraft-for-kill-web-operations-colonel-marvel-discusses-the-way-ahead-with-the-osprey/.

12

OPENING THE APERTURE ON FORCE INTEGRATION

December 11, 2023

The strategic shift from the priority on the land wars to dealing with a world of multi-polar authoritarians and a diversity of contingency operations requires significant operational change in the force.

Because MAWTS-1 is focused on standardized training for the operational force, they have an open aperture to be able to incorporate operational change but not from briefing slides and wargames, with the force that the Marines that is ready to fight tonight.

As the end of course video for WTI-1-24 opens with: "It is not a question of if the Marine Corps will go into combat, it is only a question of when."

With this perspective the future is now but done with a perspective to be able to add real capabilities wherever the Marines can find them. As one former CO of MAWTS-1 told us: "The Marines are the ultimate scavengers."

A graphic illustration for Tactical Air Control Party, Marine Aviation Weapons and Tactics Squadron One who assisted in close air support exercises during Weapons and Tactics Instructor (WTI) course 1-24, at Marine Corps Air Station Yuma, Arizona, Oct. 25, 2023. U.S. Marine Corps graphic illustration by Lance Cpl. Emily Hazelbaker.

My discussion during the November 2023 visit with Major Green who is a UH-1Y pilot Joint Terminal Attack Controller Evaluator (JTAC-E) as well as the Department Head of the Tactical Air Control Party (TACP) Department. He explained that when he first came to MAWTS, the department was called the Air Officer Department.

But this name did not reflect the reality of the personnel trained by the department. Roughly of the personnel involved are pilots and after training at MAWTS-1, the go back to their units as Forward Air Controllers.

At the completion of their time as a Forward Air Controller or Air Officer, they return to their squadron. The other half are enlisted Marines who serve as JTACs or Joint Terminal Attack Controllers.

As we talked, it was clear that the experience of the land

wars whereby JTACs controlled Close Air Support missions, although a key function, was changing as the USMC focused on maritime operations and deep interdiction missions.

How to do this shift successfully is a work in progress, but the role of the ground controllers is changing as historically they have not had access to Link-16 which is a key system for air integration and situational awareness in the Joint Force.

The C3 department has access to a variety of means to integrate data, but the challenge now is to push an ability to do similar integration to the ground controllers.

Or put in other words, legacy CAS was the focus of the ground air controller: their role now was to work as an integrative element between the GCE being distributed in the battlespace with the air element which can provide sensing, strike, and communication links for the distributed GCE.

Major Green indicated that there was an increasing focus on new simulation capability for training at MAWTS-1. The legacy systems are too limited to meet the demands for training the force for distributed and deep strike operations.

With new prototype simulation capabilities in their hands, Major Green saw the future development of LVC as an important tool in shaping a way ahead to train to new concepts of operations as well.

He noted that in his time at MAWTS-1 (nearly three years), there has been enhanced focus of attention on the maritime domain and ways the USMC operates in that domain. He noted that there was "more of a maritime flavor to our training efforts."

In short, the USMC is trying to figure out what FARPs/EABOs actually mean in the evolving combat environment, and this obviously affects the role of the TACP elements in linking together the air and the ground elements going forward.

13

THE CHALLENGES OF WORKING EXPEDITIONARY ADVANCED BASE OPERATIONS: THE PERSPECTIVE FROM THE AGS DEPARTMENT HEAD AT MAWTS-1

December During my last visit to MAWTS-1, the training effort was clearly focused on ways to enhance force mobility and lethality. There is a clear challenge in trying to determine how to position a distributed force, how to size it in order to have meaningful force capability along with enhanced survivability.

How do you position the force?

How do you organize the force?

How do deploy and move the force?

How do you find ways to reduce signature management of such a force?

In other words, at MAWTS-1, they are not wargaming Expeditionary Advanced Base Operations, they are working to determine how most effectively to do so and yet have meaningful combat effects. Not easy.

Not finished and a work in progress to determine movement, logistics support, C2 and fires solutions. It was clear when the MAGTF was the organizing principle but not so much with using EABOs as an organizational construct.

EABOs are described as follows: *Expeditionary Advanced*

Base Operations is a form of expeditionary warfare that involves the employment of mobile, low-signature, operationally relevant, and relatively easy to maintain and sustain naval expeditionary forces from a series of austere, temporary locations ashore or inshore within a contested or potentially contested maritime area in order to conduct sea denial, support sea control, or enable fleet sustainment.

EABO support the projection of naval power by integrating with and supporting the larger naval campaign. Expeditionary operations imply austere conditions, forward deployment, and projection of power.

EABO are distinct from other expeditionary operations in that forces conducting them combine various forms of operations to persist within the reach of adversary lethal and nonlethal effects.

It is critical that the composition, distribution, and disposition of forces executing EABO limit the adversary's ability to target them, engage them with fires and other effects, and otherwise influence their activities.[1]

During my visit in 2020 to MAWTS, I talked with Maj Steve Bancroft, Aviation Ground Support (AGS) Department Head, about their efforts working this problem set.

He focused on the various ways they were working enhanced force mobility, but a knotty problem was how to speed up the creation and withdrawal from EABOs.

During my 2023 visit, I continued my discussion along these lines with the current AGS Department Head, Maj Justin Atkins, a USMC combat engineer.

Atkins noted that in his deployments to date, they had not really focused on signature management. When fighting the land wars, signature management was not a key issue.

U.S. Air Force C-130 Hercules aircraft departs from a forward arming and refueling point during Assault Support Tactics 4 (AST-4), part of Weapons and Tactics Instructors (WTI) course 1-24, at Sandhill, Marine Corps Air Ground Combat Center, Twentynine Palms, California, Oct. 24, 2023. U.S. Marine Corps photo by Cpl. Alejandro Fernandez,

But when dealing with more advanced adversaries, obviously operations in the electro-magnetic spectrum had a key effect on the movement and operation of forces.

With regard to EABO, the question of how to manage forces across the combat chessboard is clearly affected by signature management and the need to organize force in ways to reduce it or to mask it. He noted that most of AGS activities are focused on FARP operations as the means to do EABOs.

They have worked multiple configurations of FARPs to do so but have not found an optimal solution. *We are building small tactical teams and exploring ways to sense, communicate, and to operate in the battlespace with mobility. But how to ensure that such teams have the desired effects?*

He noted that they work with the spectrum warfare department to do two things. First, they work with them to reduce their spectrum signature footprint. Second, they are working as well to copy that footprint to provide means to mask operations as well.

Maj Atkins noted: *Before coming to MAWTS, I never looked at the question of electromagnetic spectrum whatsoever. Now it is a central consideration of my focus and effort.*

In short, the Marines at MAWTS have been working new ways to do FARPS as a way to do EABOs, but there are key limitations to what one can do in the real world.

And ultimately, the key combat question can be put simply: What combat effect can you create with an EABO?

How does the joint force use an EABO in creating a joint effect?

And what is the relationship of the creation of EABOs to what the Marines do when the National Command Authority calls on them to deploy?

---

1. https://www.marines.mil/News/News-Display/Article/2708120/expedi tionary-advanced-base-operations-eabo/

14

REFOCUSING THE FORCE: MAWTS-1 WORKS ON WAYS AHEAD

December 14, 2023

During my visit to MAWTS-1 in November 2023, I had a chance several times to talk with the CO of the command, Col Eric Purcell, about the evolution of the three WTIs he has been in charge of since he took command.

Because I had visited in 2020, when MAWTS began to work on the shift in the USMC associated with the Commandant's guidance which has been embodied in Force Design 2030, it was quite interesting to see how MAWTS has translated that into a force that has to fight tonight.

It is not about wargaming: it is about training for combat in today's world. It is not about imaging new weapons that someday the Marines might have or working with a joint force of the future imagined by strategic planners, it is about engaging in conflict anywhere in the world when called upon to do so.

Thinking about a world with multi-polar authoritarian players does tend to focus your mind when you have to train to fight a variety of adversaries. And that is where we started our interview. Col Purcell noted that one of the major changes at the command is focusing attention on the developing capabilities of the kind of adversaries the Marines have to face.

Col Purcell as seen in the end of course video from WTI-1-24.
Credit: USMC

Purcell noted that the Marines who come to the WTIs know learn about three categories of threats: those posed by Chinese forces; those posed by Russian forces; and those posed within the context of contingency operations.

The experience of the land wars and the historical legacy of fighting against Soviet equipment does not prepare today's Marines for the conflicts in which they are engaged or likely to have to deal with. It is important to re-shape the curriculum to reflect real world dynamic threats, and Purcell noted that they were focused on doing so.

But major challenges face the Marines in doing so, and MAWTS-1 as the core warfighting training center which standardizes operational preparation needs to adapt its training approach to the evolving threat envelope.

One change which Col Purcell underscored was the need to re-focus on tac air and assault support integration. He noted that in the land wars, the two forces tended to operate somewhat in different spheres, but going forward integration was key.

In part, this is due to the range and speed requirements for a Marine Corps insertion force and the opportunity to leverage the advantages which as F-35/Osprey force provides to the USMC along with the arrival of a new generation heavy lift asset, the CH-53K.

But this also due to the changes within the assault force itself, as the Osprey adds new capabilities carried in the back of the aircraft, or its ability to contribute to new missions for the Marines such as ASW support.

A key focus of attention has been moving beyond the training to establish FARP/EABOs, to working on the more important point – what effect are you trying to create through FARP/EABOs.

With current capabilities, the Marines can create EABOs to provide for sensing capabilities, support for the transition of air elements, C2 node creation and support, but until a new generation of weapons show up, limited ability to provide for fires within a transitory EABO.

Col Purcell indicated that a primary focus within FINEX at the end of the course is bringing the different force elements together to test out their capabilities to deal with an integrated scenario.

Two scenarios were notable in our discussion.

The first was working maritime strike and support. Here the Marines would operate from Camp Pendleton with San Clemente being an enemy location which was being reinforced by red combat ships coming from the north. The U.S. Navy has provided ships for this purpose. Tac air provides the main means for interdiction of enemy shipping but simulate longer range strikes from Pendleton is involved as well.

A key capability of fifth generation aircraft is their ability to manage third party targeting which is a capability which the Marines will leverage going forward in terms of tapping into land-based strike, and one might assume this could by Army or Marine Corps ground strike capabilities.

Under the strike force, a TRAP force enabled by Ospreys operates and in FINEX, the Marines operated such a force and exercised it with the Navy and the USCG.

When the interdiction of the surface fleet threat was attenuated, the Marines shifted their attention to provide ASW support to the Navy, largely by providing sonobuoy deployment support.

A second key approach will be emphasized in next year's spring WTI.

Here the integration of TACAIR and assault support will be the focus of attention against an appropriate scenario for using such a force. With the evolution of tac air capabilities supplemented with data provided from Reapers and other ISR sources, and the evolution of the payloads carried by the assault force, a variety of scenarios can be tested in the next WTI and future WTIs.

A major challenge though facing the USMC is the dynamic changes within the joint force itself. How does the USMC support the joint force if the Navy is in the thrust of significant change sorting through what they mean by distributed maritime operations? How does the USMC support the USAF if that force is in the process of sorting out what Agile Combat Employment means in practice?

I would add that the fires challenge is a key one.

Who is the fires authority in a maritime strike scenario? A USAF air wing? A Navy surface action group?

Until this is sorted out land-based weapons whether operated by the Army or the USMC cannot have the desired effect. And having an effective joint force rests on having the fires authority challenge met and managed.

As Col Pursell concluded with this dynamic area of joint

force engagement: "Typically, we refer to Target Engagement Authority abbreviated to TEA.

"In land wars between the Combined Forces Air Component Commander (CFACC) and the Coalition Forces Land Component Command (CFLCC) we typically have this ironed out.

"But it has been such a long time since we have done true Joint Naval engagements that the process for engaging maritime targets and who exactly is the Target Engagement Authority (TEA) or can be the TEA is not as tried and true as it is for land engagements."

DR. ROBBIN F. LAIRD

A long-time analyst of global defense issues, Dr. Laird has worked in the U.S. government and several think tanks, including the Center for Naval Analysis and the Institute for Defense Analysis.

He is a Columbia University alumnus, where he taught and worked for several years at the Research Institute of International Change, a think tank founded by Dr. Brzezinski.

He is a frequent op-ed contributor to the defense press and has written several books on international security issues.

Dr. Laird has taught at Columbia University, Queens College, and Johns Hopkins University.

He has received various academic research grants as well from various foundations, including the Thyssen Foundation, the National Science Foundation. and the United States Institute for Peace.

Dr. Laird has worked for many elements of the U.S. government and with think tanks such as The Center for Defense Analysis and the Institute for Defense Analysis.

He is a member of the Board of Contributors of *Breaking Defense* and publishes there on a regular basis.

He is a frequent visitor to Australia where he is a Research Fellow with The Richard Williams Foundation in supporting their seminars on the transformation of the Australian Defence Force. He has published three books on Australian defense issues.

He is also based in Paris, France where he regularly travels throughout Europe and conducts interviews and talks with leading policy makers in the region.

OTHER SECOND LINE OF DEFENSE BOOKS OF INTEREST

All of these *Second Line of Defense* books can be purchased in e-book or paperback versions on Amazon or other on-line booksellers.

A MARITIME KILL WEB FORCE IN THE MAKING: DETERRENCE AND WARFIGHTING IN THE 21ST CENTURY

By Robbin Laird and Ed Timperlake

As Vice Admiral (Retired) Dewolfe Miller underscores: "Ultimately, peer threats are what drives change and inspires clarity in the way the Navy mans, trains, and equips its forces to defend freedom and deter aggression on a global scale. "A Maritime Kill Web Force in the Making" is the story of the evolution of the US Navy and its preparation for high-end warfare.

This is essential because the future of combat is to bring trusted and verifiable assets to the fight. The emphasis has been on connectivity, accelerated tactical decision making, as well as common equipment, that allows integration of systems within single services, across services and into allied services in a deliberate and disciplined manner. This publication provides a timely reminder of why the transformation of today's force is so necessary."

Published in 2022.

THE U.S. MARINE CORPS TRANSFORMATION PATH: PREPARING FOR THE HIGH-END FIGHT

By Robbin Laird

The United States Marine Corps began its modern transformation path after the introduction of the Osprey in 2007. In a series of in-depth interviews with the United States Marines, this analysis highlights the transformation strategy that has made the USMC one of the most dynamic military forces in the world today.

From the land wars to dealing with peer competitor threats and engagements, this book demonstrates how the Marines are navigating the strategic shift to craft innovative solutions for the return of Great Power competition.

Many coalition partners look to the USMC as a relevant benchmark for the kind of multi-domain operations which they can pursue.

For many allies, their force structure approximates the size of the USMC, and they find the fit better than emulating the total force which the United States has built.

It is also the case that the legacy force coming out of the land wars is not directly applicable in terms of its warfighting relevance to the approaches for combat with the peer competitors.

"Only time will tell how the Marine Corps navigates this treacherous transformation journey, but it's not the equipment that will make the Corps successful on the future battlefield − it's the Marines."- Lt-Gen George Trautman, USMC (Ret).

Published in 2022.

THE ROLE OF THE OSPREY IN THE PIVOT TO THE PACIFIC

By Robbin Laird

The Osprey provides an important stimulant for the shift in con-ops whereby the Navy's experimentation with distributed operations intersects with the U.S. Air Force's approach to agile combat employment and the Marine Corps' renewed interest in Expeditionary Advanced Base Operations (EABO).

In other words, the reshaping of joint and coalition maritime combat operations is underway which focuses upon distributed task forces capable of delivering enhanced lethality and survivability.

The U. S. Navy's deployed fleet — seen as the mobile sea bases they are − faces a significantly different future as part of a distributed joint force capable of shaping a congruent strike capability for enhanced lethality.

This means not only does the fleet need to operate differently in terms of its own distributed operations, but also as part of modular task forces that include air and ground elements in providing for the offensive-defensive enterprise which can hold adversaries at risk and prevail in conflict.

But how did we get here in 2023? How has the strategic shift for the joint forces evolved and caught up with what the tiltrotor revolution has enabled? And how has the Osprey evolved since the recognition of great power competition by the Trump Administration in 2018?

It began as a pivot to the Pacific in 2013; it is becoming a con-ops revolution enable in part by tiltrotor aircraft. The book takes two snapshots of this transition.

The first focuses on the introduction of the Osprey into the Pacific when the Obama Administration announced its "Pivot to the Pacific.

The second focuses on changes to the tiltrotor enterprise since 2019 after the Trump Administration highlighted the "Great Power" competition.

Published in 2023.

THE COMING OF THE CH-53K: A NEW CAPABILITY FOR THE DISTRIBUTED FORCE

By Robbin Laird

This book describes the coming of the CH-53K Kilo to the USMC and to its first international customer, the Israeli Defence Force. It is based on extensive interviews with the persons involved in the development, testing, build, and maintenance of the new combat air system.

For air system it is -- built by the digital thread development and manufacturing approach, the aircraft is designed with maintainability and fleet support in operations as a key focus of the program,

If it were called CH-55 instead of the CH-53K perhaps one would get the point that these are very different air platforms, with very different capabilities.

What they have in common, by deliberate design, is a similar logistical footprint, so that they could operate similarly off of amphibious ships or other ships in the fleet for that matter.

But the CH-53 is a mechanical aircraft, which most assuredly the CH-55 (aka as the CH-53K) is not.

In blunt terms, the CH-55 (aka as the CH-53K) is faster, carries more kit, can distribute its load to multiple locations without landing, is built as a digital aircraft from the ground up and can leverage its digital backbone for significant advancements in how it is maintained, how it operates in a task force, how it can be updated, and how it could work with unmanned systems or remotes.

These capabilities taken together create a very different lift platform than is the legacy CH-53E. In a strategic environment where force mobility is informing capabilities across the combat spectrum, it is hard to understate the value of a lift platform, notably one which can talk and operate digitally, in carving out new tactical capabilities with strategic impacts.

The lift side of the equation within a variety of environments can be stated succinctly. The King Stallion will lift 27,000 lbs. external payload, deliver it 110 nm to a high-hot zone, loiter, and return to the ship with fuel to spare.

What that means is JLTV's (22,600-lb.), up-armored HMMWV, and other heavier tactical cargos go to shore by air, rather than by LCAC or other slower sea lift means. For less severe ambient conditions or shorter distances than this primary mission, the 53K can carry up to 36,000 lbs.

With ever increasing lift requirements and advancing threats in the battlefield, there is no other vertical lift aircraft available that meets emerging heavy lift needs.

There are a lot of platforms that can blow things up or kill people, but for heavy lift, the CH-53K is the only option. The digital piece is a foundational element and why it is probably better thought of as a CH-55. This starts with the fly-by-wire flight controls. The CH-53K is the first and only heavy lift fly-by-wire helicopter.

The CH-53K's fly-by-wire is a leap in technology from legacy mechanical flight control systems and keeps safety and survivability at the core of the Kilo's design while providing a portal to an optionally piloted capability and autonomy.

The CH-53K's fly-by-wire design drastically reduces pilot

workload and minimizes exposure to threats or danger, particularly during complex missions or challenging aircraft maneuvers like low light level externals in a degraded visual environment allowing the pilot to manage and lead the mission vice focusing on physically controlling the aircraft.

What this means is that the CH-53K "can operate and fight on the digital battlefield."

And because the flight crew are enabled by the digital systems onboard, they can focus on the mission rather than focusing primarily on the mechanics of flying the aircraft.

This will be crucial as the Marines shift to using unmanned systems more broadly than they do now.

Published in 2023.

MY FIFTH-GENERATION JOURNEY: 2004-2018

By Robbin Laird

Tis is the first of two books looking at the standup of the F-35 global enterprise.

According to the author: "It is my personal journey observing the development and evolution of the aircraft from my time working with the man who coined the term fifth-generation aircraft, Michael W. Wynne, through my many visits to F-35 sites, interviews with pilots, maintainers, and U.S. and allied government officials who navigated through the incredibly negative press and government officials trying to kill the program to have delivered a unique capability in the history of combat aircraft."

"It is a personal journey and I take the reader to many of the places where I went to talk with the F-35 nation. But I did so not only in the United States but in the nations of key members of the F-35 global enterprise. My journey is unique and I tell it not because of a desire to be remembered but in playing a role of recorder of history of those members of the military of many nations who made this capability real despite the media and many government officials desires to see them fail."

"But failure would have meant that we would have had even less capability than we have now after 20 years of fighting in wars of "stability" which have brought us the opposite."

As LtGen George Trautman, USMC (Ret), Former USMC Deputy Commandant for Aviation, writes in the forward to the book:

"Robbin's ability to capture the perspectives of the key players, from pilots to maintainers and logisticians, provides a comprehensive and insightful account of this revolutionary aircraft.

"Moreover, the book uncovers the geopolitical implications of Fifth-Generation warfighting capabilities. As nations seek to assert their dominance and secure their interests, the strategic implications of these technologies ripple across the global stage.

"Through a series of personal essays and skilled interviews with those who understand the aircraft, *My Fifth-Generation Journey: 2004-2018* deftly navigates through this complex web, painting a vivid picture of how Fifth-Generation warfighting will shape the future geopolitical landscape."

The book includes a number of original photos shot by the author during his visits highlighting the roles of pioneers in the setting up of the F-35 in the services and abroad.

The book was published in 2023.

APPENDIX

RECOLLECTIONS ON THE ESTABLISHMENT OF MAWTS-1

December 6, 2023

By Howard DeCastro, LtCol USMC, (Ret.)

Trying to describe how MAWTS-1 and the WTI training concept began is very much like the classic tale of the blind men describing an elephant. After Vietnam, there were lots of Marines who were thinking about ways to improve Marine Corps Aviation and there were many initiatives throughout the Marine Corps. Everyone who participated in the establishment of MAWTS-1 and the development of the Weapons and Tactics (WTI) concept has a slightly different story.

This article presents my recollections.

In 1976 I was stationed at NAS Miramar, scheduled to be the Executive Officer of the first Marine Corps F-14 Squadron. When the Marine Corps decided the F-14 was the wrong fighter for the Marine Corps and canceled its participation, Colonel Bob Norton, Commanding Officer of MCCRTG-10, asked me to come to MCCRTG-10 in Yuma, Arizona. After closing down the Marine Command at MCAS Miramar, I transferred to MCAS Yuma with several of the Pilots and Radar Intercept Officers who had been part of the F-14 Program and a few of us went to work on building an F-4 Training Program using the Instructional Systems Development (ISD) construct that was used to develop the F-14 Classroom Training System.

Captains Rick Scivicque, Rob Savio, Jim Hollopeter, Jerry Cross and I put together an F-4 ISD based training system with funding from Jim Bolwerk, a retired Naval Aviator, who was heading up the Navy's Training Directorate at COMNAVAIRPAC. The funding went through the Aviation Training Department at Headquarters Marine Corps and was supported by Colonel Paul Boozman. Colonel Boozman would have preferred development of a Helicopter Training Program, but the money was controlled by COMNAVAIRPAC and was earmarked for Navy and Marine Corps F-4 use.

Colonel Boozman knew that Marine Corps helicopter training was in need of a more standardized, focused, and formal program that would teach the tactics and skills necessary for force projection in combat. I emphasize this point because his strong position on the need for improved tactical training for the Helicopter community helped ensure the inclusion of helicopter training and, broadly, inclusion of training for all aviation assets in the development of the MAWTS/WTI concept.

While working on the F-4 ISD project Colonel Norton and his XO Colonel John Hudson made us aware of Project 19, one of the many recommendations on ways to improve Marine Corps Combat Readiness that then Colonel John Cox presented to the Commandant. Colonel Norton directed us to put together a concept of how Marine Corps Aviation training could be improved.

Over the next year, working with people like Bill Bauer (CO of VMFAT-101), Bobby Butcher (XO and then CO of VMAT-102), Dave Vest (XO then CO of VMFA-531 and previous head of the F-4 shop in MAWTU-PAC), we put together our ideas and developed the MAWTS/WTI concept.

Collectively, we had not been satisfied with the application of air power in Vietnam, our only war experience. There were numerous tactical applications that were effective (A-6 strikes in the north; close air support; helicopter troop insert, withdrawal, and rescue; C-130 tactical resupply; and breaking the siege of Khe San are examples).

However, an overall strategy, the integration of aviation

resources, and effective coordination with the ground elements was less than ideal. It was clear we lost more Marines than we should have because we were not well coordinated with the Ground Forces and weren't well coordinated with other squadrons, especially with other types of fixed wing, helicopter, and transport aircraft squadrons.

In the 1960s and 1970s, Fleet Squadron training depended on the quality of the more experienced pilots and whether they would teach what they knew or just try to beat you and hope you would learn. The Special Weapons Training Units and later MAWTUPAC and MAWTULANT had good Attack and Fighter training and certification programs that helped the A-6, A-4 and F-4 communities standardize and improve their training and combat capability, but these were generally specific to the aircraft type and didn't integrate the full range of aviation types and capabilities. The Navy's "Top Gun" school that started in the 1970's was excellent for the improvement of individual Air Combat Maneuvering (ACM) skills but was available only to F-4 fighter crews.

Integrated training with the Marine Corps Ground Forces was also less than optimum. While there were opportunities to participate in some Ground Training Scenarios, the lack of participation in planning and debriefing led to exercises that failed to build the kind of integrated support that is necessary to be highly effective in combat.

We developed a concept that would include all aviation assets, working together as a coordinated and integrated team, to support a Ground Scheme of Maneuver. We fully understood that the value of the Marine Corps was invested in the troops on the ground who could defeat the enemy and take and occupy the terrain that is critical for winning battles and wars and knew it was our job to provide the best possible air support to enhance their combat capability.

While we were working on the concept at MCAS Yuma

and El Toro, California, there were other Marines throughout the Corps who were developing similar and alternative concepts. It was clear the Marine Corps was going to do something significant to improve the training and application of our aviation assets. It remained to know where, what, and when.

Key elements of our concept were:

- The inclusion and integration of all Marine Corps aviation assets, every type of tactical aircraft, command and control, logistics, and air defense.
- Each year, train one pilot/aircrew from each squadron in the Marine Corps as Weapons and Tactics Instructors (WTIs) who would act as instructors and operations coordinators in their squadrons. Assign those pilots/aircrew back to their squadron for three, or at least a minimum of two years so that, once established, every squadron would have two WTI pilots/aircrews.
- Provide ground training on individual aircraft and the broad range of Marine Corps aviation assets to learn how to integrate and utilize the capabilities of the full range of Marine Aviation to support the Marine Corps Ground forces.
- Provide individual and combined-force flight training utilizing the best-known tactics for air combat and defensive combat maneuvering, ground attack, close air support, troop insertion, logistics supply, electronic warfare, command-and-control, and reconnaissance.
- Provide instruction on the capabilities of our known and potential enemies and the best tactics to defeat them.

Some senior officers thought the Command of MAWTS should be restricted to Fighter Pilots. We thought it important to share command of MAWTS among the communities to ensure broad buy-in of the concept, and recommended that the Commanding Officer shift from fixed wing to helicopter aviators every other change of command.

We also recommended that the incoming Commanding Officer should serve one year as Executive Officer to ensure a smooth transition from Commanding Officer to Commanding Officer, like the "Fleet-up" construct used in Navy Squadrons.

We didn't alternate Command immediately because we had not brought a Helicopter pilot in as Executive Officer and thought it important that the next Commanding Officer be someone who was thoroughly familiar with the background and goals of MAWTS/WTI.

I recommended that Bobby Butcher be my relief because he was a proven leader, had helped develop the concept, fully understood what we were trying to do, had a successful Squadron Command, and could easily take over and maintain the momentum we had established.

Colonel Butcher cemented the practice of rotating the Command between fixed and rotary wing aviators and the Fleet-up construct by selecting Jake Vermilyea, a transport and helicopter pilot as his Executive Officer and eventual replacement as the third Commanding Officer of MAWTS-1. Colonel Butcher did this even though there was significant push-back from some Senior Fighter Pilots. It helped that LtGen White, a Helicopter pilot, was the Deputy Commandant for Aviation and supported Colonel Butcher's position.

It is an understatement to say that not all Marine Aviators supported the MAWTS/WTI concept. Many thought it was far too expensive. There was significant push back on the inclusion of helicopters and transports based on the fear that the current MAWTU programs supporting A-6, A-4, and F-4 training would be watered down. There also was concern about Yuma as the location. Notably, Colonel John Ditto, Legislative Assistant to the Commandant, who had been the head of the F-4 Fighter Shop in MAWTULANT and was familiar with the ranges on the east coast, thought the new unit should be stationed out of Beaufort or Cherry Point.

The concept we put together in Yuma was pitched at a conference held at El Toro, chaired by Colonel Don Gillam of FMFPAC. Although some of the conference attendees did not fully support the concept as presented, Colonel Gillam deemed the conference enough of a success that he sent LtGen Andy O'Donnel, Commanding General FMFPAC, a message that FMFPAC should support the concept.

As a result of LtGen O'Donnel's support, LtGen Tom Miller, Deputy Commandant for Aviation, asked for a briefing. LtCol Bill Cooper who was at HQMC AAP, presented the brief that we had developed and LtGen Miller approved the concept.

Concurrently, at Headquarters Marine Corps, a great deal of thought and planning had gone into the development of improved Aviation Training. Parallel with the development of our MAWTS/WTI concept, there was an initiative to merge the two MAWTUs.

The HQMC initiative and the MAWTS/WTI concept fit well together. A decision was made to have the new unit report to Aviation Training, where Colonel Paul Boozman was influential. His vision, direction, and support were important in forming MAWTS-1, from gaining support from the Commandant, providing the funding, approving the manning, and choosing the location.

It was decided to conduct a trial course under the direction of the MAWTUs. MAWTUPAC under LtCol Ray Hanle was selected to lead the effort. Instructors from the two MAWTUs, augmented by other highly respected pilots and crew members presented the first Weapons and Tactics Instructor (WTI) course in 1977. The course was enough of a success that a second trial class was conducted in early 1978. The success of those two WTI classes led to establishment and Commissioning of Marine Aviation Weapons and Tactics Squadron-One (MAWTS-1) in June of 1978 with 35 officers and 19 enlisted Marines.

In researching this article, I have been reminded that there was a trial course held by MAWTULANT on the East Coast. That course apparently was not as well received as those held at Yuma, which helped cement the decision for Yuma as the best location.

A great deal of credit for the successful initiation of the MAWTS/WTI concept lies with Colonel Hanle and the MAWTU instructors who conducted those two first trial courses.

Much of the early success of MAWTS-1 came from the steady support of Colonel Boozman at Headquarters Marine Corps Aviation Training, and from LtCol Duane Wills in the Officer Assignment Branch. Colonel Boozman was instrumental in shaping the concept, and supporting and approving the training and command constructs, ensuring MAWTS-1 was fully staffed, and that it was adequately funded.

During my two years with MAWTS-1 we conducted four WTI Courses. Support from the Air Wings was excellent, and support from VMAT-102 and VMFAT-101 was outstanding, providing maintenance support and even aircraft when required.

There are some interesting stories about those first two years, such as the MAWTS-1 CH-53 Instructors being pulled out to support the training for the Iranian Hostage Rescue, a trip to Israel to confer with the leaders of the Entebbe Rescue, a Final Exercise evolution that was conducted in marginal weather, and the unfortunate loss of a CH-46 with Crew and passengers and loss of an F-4 Crew.

Near the end of my tenure, General Wilson, Commandant of the Marine Corps, visited the command for a briefing. In that brief I raised some issues of concern about the mobility of Command and Control, lack of armament for helicopters, and paucity of anti-air capability. While this was not the brief General Wilson had expected, it led to MAWTS being tied in with the Deputy for Aviation for discussion, participation, and influence on a variety of aviation issues.

I have had the pleasure of visiting MAWTS-1 several times since I retired in 1980. It appears that every Commanding Officer, with the support of the excellent MAWTS-1 Staff, has improved its value to the Marine Corps. The direct involvement of Secretary Lehman helped bring MAWTS-1 training to a higher level. MAWTS-1 has grown in size, mission depth, and overall capability.

We thought, when it first began, that Marine Corps Aviation would be improved and that someday most, if not all, Wing Commanders would be former MAWTS Instructors and/or WTIs which would certainly improve the coordination, integration, and combat capabilities of Marine Air. That has happened. The Marine Corps has even had a Commandant who was a MAWTS-1 Instructor.

The author was the first commander of MAWTS-1.

USMC DEPLOYMENT ONBOARD HMS QUEEN ELIZABETH: THE PARTNERSHIP WHICH ALMOST DID NOT HAPPEN

October 18, 2020

In this September 23, 2020 story published by 3rd Marie Aircraft Wing, the historic deployment of USMC F-35Bs onboard the UK's largest warship ever built by the UK was highlighted.[1]

PORTSMOUTH, England — Marine Fighter Attack Squadron 211 embarked 10 F-35B Lightning II Joint Strike Fighters onboard Her Majesty's Ship Queen Elizabeth, September 22, as part of the squadron's multi-month deployment for training to the United Kingdom. "The Wake Island Avengers" are proud to represent the United States Marine Corps and United States of America while they serve as part of the UK's Carrier Strike Group.

"HMS Queen Elizabeth will be operating with the largest air group of 5th generation fighters assembled anywhere in the world," said Commodore Steve Moorhouse, Commander UK CSG. "Led by the Royal Navy, and backed by our closest allies, this new Carrier Strike Group puts real muscle back into NATO; and sends a clear signal that the United Kingdom takes its global role seriously."

VMFA-211 joined the UK's 617 Squadron "The Dambusters" onboard the 65,000-ton carrier as she sailed for exercises with NATO allies in the North Sea. This month's overarching UK-led Group Exercise will see VMFA-211, 617 Squadron and HMS Queen Elizabeth joined by six Royal Navy destroyers, frigates and auxiliaries, ready to fight in any clime or place.

In addition to these forces, the UK CSG will be joined by warships from the Royal Netherlands Navy and US Navy to form the largest UK-led multi-national force in recent years, which will accompany HMS Queen Elizabeth on her global, inaugural deployment in 2021.

"This is the Special Relationship in action," said Robert Wood Johnson, U.S. ambassador to the United Kingdom. "Our forces train, fight, and win – side by side – to protect our two countries."

Before the deployment, the CSG will be put through its paces off the north east coast of Scotland as part of Joint Warrior, NATO's largest annual exercise. Joint Warrior will be an opportunity for the CSG to exercise the capabilities of 15 5th generation F-35Bs flown by VMFA-211 and Squadron 617.

The F-35B combines next-generation fighter characteristics of radar-evading stealth, sensor fusion, fighter agility and advanced logistical support with the most powerful and comprehensive integrated sensor package of any fighter aircraft in history, providing unprecedented lethality and access to highly contested environments.

"During this special partnership, the US Marine Corps and US Navy will conduct carrier strike group operations, training to maritime power projection, and ultimately supporting shared security," said Doran. "Our alliance is stronger because we can deploy and fight together as truly integrated NATO allies."

This exercise is a historic moment for the United Kingdom and the United States which strengthens the special relationship between the two countries. For the UK, it will be the largest air group to operate from a Royal Navy carrier since HMS Hermes in 1983; as well as the next step leading toward HMS Queen Elizabeth's worldwide deployment this spring.

For the United States, it is the first time a squadron of 5th generation aircraft will be deployed aboard a foreign vessel and will prove that the "Wake Island Avengers" are ready to conduct operations in support of NATO.

The "Wake Island Avengers" made history in 2018 when the squadron completed the first F-35B combat deployment, successfully supporting ground operations in Central Command's area of responsibility.

"The Wake Island Avengers are ready in all respects to work with the British sailors and aircrew onboard HMS Queen Elizabeth," said Lt. Col. Joseph Freshour, the commanding officer of VMFA-211. "We are looking forward to deploying alongside our British counterparts."

VMFA-211 deployed for training to Royal Air Force Station Marham in the early evening of September 3. The pilots flew from Marine Corps Air Station Yuma, Arizona to MCAS Beaufort, South Carolina, and then onto RAF Mahram, a distance of 5500 nautical miles. Since then, VMFA-211 has been conducting realistic, relevant training at RAF Marham with "The Dambusters."

While serving as part of the UK Carrier Strike Group, VMFA-211 will use innovative techniques to combine efforts and resources while collaborating on complex mission sets to maintain our Nations' global maritime military advantage. The Navy-Marine Corps team is humbled and proud to represent the United States and continue the special relationship with the United Kingdom in support of shared security.

But looking back, this partnership almost did not happen.

10 years ago this month, the UK government announced that they were pulling out from the F-35B program to buy F-35Cs, and to redesign their new carriers to use catapults, namely, the new electronic catapults planned by the US Navy for the USS Ford class.

As part of the UK's 2010 strategic review, the government committed to rebuilding their new carriers to enable "cats and traps" as the launch mechanism, and the purchase of F-35Cs versus F-35Bs.

This decision left the USMC in a very difficult situation within the Pentagon at the time, ramping up pressure on their F-35B purchases.

Suggestive of the position the UK decision to move to the C versus the B put the Marines in is found in the analysis in this March 26, 201 article by Robert F. Dorr:

"New details have emerged about plans for the "mix" of F-35B and F-35C Lightning II Joint Strike Fighters (JSF) that the U. S. Marine Corps will operate. At the same time, some in Washington are questioning whether the short take-off/vertical landing (STOVL) F-35B version may be in jeopardy.

"Gen. James F. "Tamer" Amos, commandant of the Marine Corps, defends the F-35B, but acknowledges that its future is less clear than it once was. With their emphasis on ship-to-shore operations, the Marines have an enormous stake in STOVL, but in Washington some question whether the F-35B is worth the investment.

"Doubts arose about the viability of the F-35B before Britain dropped its plans for the STOVL version. Still, a major defense downsizing in the United Kingdom sharply reduces the number of the STOVL aircraft on order. Britain once wanted 150 F-35Bs, reduced the number to 138, and subsequently shifted to the F-35C carrier-based model in an economy move that also involves redesign of the first of two 65,000-ton Queen Elizabeth-class carriers.

"The only other committed user, Italy, wants 22 F-35Bs for its navy aircraft carriers, and 40 more for its air force. Observers in both Washington and Rome, however, are wondering whether the 40 air force aircraft will be built. If not, overall purchases of the STOVL F-35B would be cut in half at a time when questions about cost persist."[2]

As Lt. General (Retired) George Trautman put it today:

"Within days of the UK decision, the Commandant and I found ourselves in a fight for the mere existence of the F-35B.

"The program's opponents in the US Navy, OSD and Congress, urged on by a false narrative from industry, were almost gleeful that we appeared to be isolated.

"Thankfully, we were able to defend the program and my prediction that the UK would return to STOVL turned out to be right just two years later."

Now there are several F-35B users globally, with the prospect of others, precisely for the reason the USMC bought it, namely, deployment flexibility.

Lt. General (Retired) George Trautman added to his comment made today (October 18, 2020):

"Today, the the unique capabilities of the F-35B are widely recognized and the aircraft has been embraced by a growing number of nations.

Watching VMFA-211 and UK's 617 Squadron operate

side-by-side on the HMS Queen Elizabeth is a wonderful endorsement of STOVL and the special relationship that exists between the two countries."

As fixed airfields become higher risk propositions, an ability of an aircraft to fly from a wide variety of sites which can operate as airfields in a crisis, has become not a nice to have capability but a necessary one.

But by 2012, the UK government did a U-turn and recommitted to the F-35B.

The UK Defence Secretary at the time of the reversal, Philip Hammond noted:

"Carrier strike with 'cats and traps' using the carrier variant jet no longer represents the best way of delivering carrier strike and I am not prepared to tolerate a three-year further delay to reintroducing our carrier strike capability.

"This announcement means we remain on course to deliver carrier strike in 2020 as a key part of our Future Force 2020."

The estimated cost of fitting the "cats and traps" system to HMS Prince of Wales had risen from £950m to £2bn "with no guarantee that it will not rise further".

But, he revealed, the government had spent between £40m and £50m on design and assessment work and there would also be penalty costs associated with scrapping the F-35C deal.[3]

Well it is 2020 and Hammond was right.

But then again so were we.

Ed Timperlake published a piece on March 16, 2012, which highlighted the UK reversal and forecast why he thought this was the right decision. And when one looks at the Marines onboard the HMS Queen Elizabeth his forecast proved very accurate indeed.

March 16, 2012

by Ed Timperlake

The UK is rethinking its carrier aircraft decision.

In large part this is because of the cost necessary to build traps and cats on the Queen Elizabeth class carrier.

In part it is because of the impact of Libya and Bold Alligator in reminding strategists and decision-makers of the flexibility provided for deck management and fleet operations of a V/STOL aircraft.

In this article, I am going to take a look at the logic of shifting from the C to the B and how it fits evolving technologies and operational dynamics. I would argue that both technologically and operationally moving back to the B makes great sense as the UK shapes its evolving military capabilities.

And indeed a F-35B and F-35A combination provides a significant opportunity to bring the RAF and the Royal Navy on the same page **with both** contributing to a UK ESG construct and approach.

Looking Back at UK History

When England went to war to stop Hitler, Sir Winston Churchill was immediately appointed First Lord of the Admiralty and the signal went out to the Royal Navy—"Winston is Back."

This was the beginning of the greatest Sea war in the history of the world. The Royal Navy at first standing alone would learn invaluable lessons paid for in blood on how to fight and win. The costs were high; tragically ship design defects were uncovered in the crucible of combat.

For example, the loss of the Royal Navy Battle Cruiser Hood was a faulty design in armor because of vulnerability to plunging shells and also the Hood's ammo locker igniting was a contributing fact. Then, during the pursuit of Bismarck the HMS Ark Royal, a British aircraft carrier, launched "Swordfish" bi-planes and with a single torpedo took out the Bismarck's rudder and sealed it's doom.

The shift from battleships to aircraft carriers was dramatic. The HMS Repulse and Prince of Wales fighting alone against Japanese planes without friendly air cover were both lost off Singapore right after the US Navy had its Battleship Fleet sunk pier side by a Japanese carrier air attack at Pearl Harbor.

World War II demonstrated that evolving and innovative tactics, training and technology were needed to fight battles from the Arctic into the southern hemisphere over the expanse of two oceans.

This global ocean war created a tactical and technology partnership between the US Navy and Royal Navy that continues strong to this day. After the war, with the advent of jet engines and the growth of aircraft carries into "super carriers," the relationship was deepened.

The contribution of the Royal Navy is heard in every cockpit coming on board a USN carrier on every landing "Meat Ball — Line-up — Angel of Attack" is the scan pattern all USN/USMC Carrier Pilots. That mantra is taught from day one on a Naval Aviators quest to successfully Carrier Qual (CQ) in order to receive their Navy Wings of Gold and join a squadron ready for sea duty. This lifesaving mantra is built on several design gifts given to the US Navy by the Royal Navy.

Centering the "meat ball" puts the aircraft on a perfect glide slope for an "OK-3 wire" the code for a perfect trap. Calling -the "meat ball" to the LSO, along with fuel state, is possible because of the evolution of the fresnel lens which the British pioneered for their early jet carrier operations.

"Line-up." adjusting for the centerline, is now targeted to align with an angled deck. That design added a huge margin of safety. The angle deck also greatly aided efficient operations during flight quarters effectively to cycle Carrier Air Group (CAG) aircraft into an effective unified airborne fighting force.

Finally, checking the " Angle Of Attack" is an easy and fail safe indicator of having sufficient and safe airspeed to come aboard.

The British also designed the "hurricane bow" because a modern carrier must be sea worthy from the Arctic to the Equator with the ability to operate in all weather, day and night. Sea worthiness against a "cruel sea" is critical and the British got it right as Carrier Aviation transitioned from props to jets. Finally, thanks again to the Royal Navy for steam catapults to give added energy for a successful carrier take off of high performance jets.

It is fair to say that operating day or night, in all weather from ice to tropics, a modern aircraft carrier is one of the most complex engineering achievements of any society. It transports thousands of sailors across all oceans, escorted by support ships and aircraft — all with a mission to project power. 4.5 Acres of sovereign US airfield capable of 30+ knots going into harms way is a significant combat asset.

Shaping the Next Round of Naval Aviation and Operational Concepts

The entire *raison-d'etre* of a modern aircraft carrier is the composition of carrier air wing.

From Korea to Vietnam, to Desert Storm and today's fight a US Aircraft Carrier, like "The Big E" (the USS Enterprise), has a an airwing of aircraft that always has had "generation parity" with any peer competitor flying from land bases. The air wing also had electronic warfare aircraft and flying command and control aircraft. The USN angle deck carrier and aircraft all came together to dominate any potential sea threat and also successfully carry the fight "feet dry" in current modern combat.

The British during the period of super carrier supremacy were pioneering the tactical employment of the AV-8 Harrier from decks that did not need "cats and traps" to operate.

Although the V/STOL Harrier was limited, it was very ready and effective in an air-to-ground role and had some modest, but when absolutely needed, fleet saving capabilities in the Falkland Campaign, in the fighter air-to-air role.

But in a never-ending action-reaction cycle of technology improvements, a V/STOL aircraft has emerged which is a significant advance for naval aviation. The F-35 not only will be a successful air-to-ground fighter but also an air-to-air fighter and an EW fighter combined.

The F-35 is not a linear performance enhancement from F/A-18 4th Gen; it has a third performance axis — "Z" The "Z" axis is the pilot's cockpit C4ISR-D "OODA" loop axis.

The design characteristics blended together prior to F-35 have been constantly improving range, payload (improved by system/and weapons carried), maneuverability (measured by P Sub s), useful speed, and range (modified by V/STOL—a plus factor).

The F-35 is also designed with inherent survivability factors-first redundancy and hardening and then stealth.

Stealth is usually seen as the 5th Gen improvement. But reducing the F-35 to a linear x-y axis improvement or to stealth simply misses the point.

Traditionally, the two dimensional depiction is that the y-axis is time and the x-axis captures individual airplanes that tend to cluster in generation improvement.

Each aircraft clustered in a "generation" is a combination of improvements.

Essentially, the aeronautical design "art" of blending together ever improving and evolving technology eventually creates improvements in a linear fashion.

The F-35 is now going to take technology into a revolutionary three-dimensional situational awareness capability.

F-35B Landing on the USS Wasp October 2011 Credit: SLD

This capability establishes a new vector for TacAir aircraft design.

This can be measured on a "Z" axis.

What makes this possible is the F-35B has both a fully up air-to-air and air-to-ground capability. In the AA mode it is supersonic and stealthy with the same "Z-axis" revolutionary C4ISR-D cockpit that Navy F-35Cs and AF −F-35As both have. Consequently, the F-35B can fit seamlessly into the Air Force/Navy Air Dominance mission.

Historically, air fleet command and control, now C^5ISR, was external to 1,2,3, and 4th Generations TacAir. C &C goals were to enhance fleet wide combat performance for all Type/Model/Series (T/M/S) of TacAir.

This is the modern AWACS , Hawkeye and Aegis battle concept.

Now using a three-dimensional graph the "Z-axis" research takes airpower into a totally different domain. The shift is from externally provided C&C to C5ISR-D in the cockpit carried by the individual air platform.

This is the revolutionary step function that breaks the linear progression of previous Generations.

THE EXECUTION OF THE TRAP MISSION OVER LIBYA

One of the training missions being worked at MAWTS-1 with the increased focus on maritime operations has been upon the TRAP mission.

Already in the Libyan operations, the Osprey demonstrated its unique qualities in performing this mission.

Now MAWTS-1 is working to standardize the training for this important mission set.

But let us look back at that mission executed in Libya.

September 25, 2011

During a Second Line of Defense visit to New River to discuss Osprey operations and experiences with the Osprey Nation, we had a chance to discuss the TRAP mission over Libya with the ACE commander and with one of the Osprey operators involved in the mission. Earlier we discussed this mission with the MEU commander.

In this interview Maj. B.J. Debardeleben discussed the mission after take off from the ship off of the coast of Libya.

After we took off, the autopilot took over. That is one of the great things on this plane versus the SEA KNIGHT is that it can fly itself through part of the operation. In a car, if you can set speed control, you can now be able to use your mind and do something else and focus on the road. And it's exactly what we did on the plane and you're monitoring the flying, but now you're able to manage the mission better.

We were focusing on shaping our way to the moving recovery zone. We compared the mission plan to the unfolding operation. Let's look at this, figure out some more things, and to make sure everything's right that we did with our mission planning before we left the boat. So it gave us time to assess everything with the radio, talk to people we needed to, and build our situational awareness.

We immediately started talking to the Harrier operating above us. And he starts talking with the pilot and we can hear one side of the conversation and I can tell that things are getting worse on the ground.

We made the judgment that we had to accelerate the mission. We moved towards our top speed as the pilot was moving to a new location on the ground.

The pilot on the ground indicated that "they're still going at us, and things are getting worse." And he is clearly on the move.

We had the grid of the plane crash site and we got a new grid and realized that it was much further away from where the original crash site was. So he'd been on the move the whole time.

If I had been flying a SEA KNIGHT, by the time I had gotten the new information with regard to the shift in the grid, and flown for the 40 minutes under those conditions, I would have been relatively exhausted by the time I got there because you're holding the controls, and you're getting shaken the whole time.

On the Osprey, I am on autopilot. So I can take a sip of water, I'm assessing everything, and I'm listening to what's going on very clearly. The V22s very quiet in airplane mode so we can hear the radios very well, but if I was in a SEA KNIGHT the noise would make it difficult to hear. The grunts in the back were able to look at a moving map that they can look at to have both SAs when we're getting closer and closer to coast line.

And so in that flight task now they're relaxed and comfortable instead of them shaking in the back because usually with all the shaking makes you groggy you sleep, so you have to wake them up when you land. So they're in the back at least relaxed and calm before we drop them off.

We zoom all the way in, we get about ten miles off the coast, I drop down from 500 feet to about 200, 300, feet just to stabilize radars. Looking at the coastline, and I was expecting Libya to look Djibouti which presents a very dark profile. But it was light up, with the electricity grid.

And so we just picked a dark spot. We also had a visual map. So now I'm looking at where I'm going to fly, I look at it on the map and I say, "I'm going through there."

Another thing I didn't have in the SEA KNIGHT was that actual navigation. I had been holding a map with a flashlight trying to figure stuff out while the other person's flying and shaking and you got to be able to do this without knowing where you're going. With the terrain guidance you can make a rapid assessment of the terrain and how you are going to fly over that terrain.

Where you're in a V22 you look at it and you get all the data right in front of you. It's basically like having a smart phone versus using a dial telephone. All these things are helping you out in a difficult situation.

So they give me a new grid, and I'm looking for my needle, to where I'm supposed to go, a large town, and then I'll look outside and I see a large town full of lights and probably that was an area the downed pilot was running from.

So I adjust my course a little bit to the left, go through the dark area, and then come through. I'm seeing pilot lines; I can mark all sorts of things on my map.

I'm flying inbound, the Harrier has built a picture for me, and he's talking to me, telling me what I'm going to see, what the road looks like, where he is. Gives me that updated grid.

The F15 and F16 are now back on station and they start talking. They're doing a good job of talking to the downed pilot and they know who he is, you know, they're friends with him. They encourage him to have a drink of water and to calm down and to just stay where we was now.

Earlier, there was commotion going on at the response station, there's people chasing him, and there's cars chasing him. The Harrier used various means to kind of scare people away from him. That's when he said," say good bye to my wife". I could hear in my guy's voice that things were getting more serious.

One nice thing also about having people overhead is that they are in calmer environment able to look at the situation and give you more information. "Hey Ospreys, you guys have DF?" They said " we have DF," so they put it up, and cue somebody one, two, three, four, five, that other needle swings over on top of my navigation needle, now saying that he's generally in that area that you're headed towards.

The joint quality of the operation is important. One of the best things I think about it is, that we are joint enough in terminology and techniques and everything all relatively the same. You know, we may have differences that are minute, but our terminology is all the same and we can interop wherever we have to in such a situation

In fact, I learned later that we went to introductory aviation school together in Pensacola. When I went down to visit him in the hospital, we realized that we went to school together at Pensacola. You just never get how small the world's going to get when somebody comes back from 11 years ago.

So we're coming in. One of the other best things about the Osprey is so, besides it being comfortable for us, it is quiet on the outside in airplane mode. Nobody's going to hear us until we've gone past them. And it just sounds like a whisper rush. And at night you're not going to know anything about it. The SEA KNIGHT or any helicopter, you are hearing it from 10 to 15 miles away, you're not going to hear anything from us until we're at least beyond you.

But as I'm coming in, I hear him, he's very quiet at this point, and I can hear the dogs barking in the background starting in my mind to envision where he is and what's going on. And they're talking about the vehicles pushing northwest and nobody knows where he is at that point, so it's looking good. And so we're all starting out thinking about where we're going to land. And that zone wasn't described as to what the surface was. He just said land it by this road.

We have an inertial navigation system, so get when I say plot of our plane in time and space. And so if we set up to land, we get a velocity vector that shows our movement on the earth and you don't have to look outside to land.

And it's an awesome capability because when the helo goes up, if you look at it and you look at gusts and the way it flows, it looks like it's moving. Your helo is going backwards and it becomes very confusing for the helicopter pilot. And it's always been one of the hardest things for us to do is land in the desert safely.

And in the Osprey they have fixed it. We can do this manually looking at the system, or the plane can fly itself to hover, and land directly down, you know, no questions asked, and it is amazing; both ways work 100 percent of the time.

94

As we're coming to land we start to turn into a helicopter and we're setting up to land. And as soon as we speed the motor blades up and then started bringing out, the noise comes on. And it is loud.

And as soon as I do that, the downed pilot starts yelling on the radio, he's like "Don't leave me, I hear you." And I was like, "Hey we got it, we know where you are, we're coming, you know, send your flare up."

So he sends his signal early, it's a high light night, very bright, a few clouds in the sky; it was just really not good for such a mission to go down. I get over him as he's starting to talk as my crew chief finally says, you know, "I see him."

We get a sparkle of the F16 and marks the spot. My guy comes in and lands right beside him, we're pretty much about 20 feet away from him. He jumps up, hands up, you know, no sign of radio or pistol or anything, he said he never even pulled his pistol out of his holster the whole time.

He runs to the plane, pretty much jumps on, and sits down and puts on his seat belt and he's like, "I'm ready to go." The grunts spread out, to secure the zone for a second. Crew chief runs out there and grabs him, says everybody get back on the plane.

As I'm coming around I ask, "Do you have him on board?" I am told "Yup, my guy's on."

Because I am the second Osprey accompanying the one, which landed, I don't even land I kind of come up beside him, I keep going, they pick up and then all together we leave.

The success of the mission was due in part to significant training. We trained for seven months as a team to do this. And then every time we had a chance on a boat in Djibouti or wherever we were, we trained to TRAP also. Because it's the one way we can get the grunts on the back of the plane where we can use the jets overhead to work together and then land in the zone.

APPENDIX

1. https://www.marines.mil/News/News-Display/Article/2360600/first-f-35b-deployment-aboard-partner-nation-vessel/.
2. https://www.defensemedianetwork.com/stories/marine-f-35b-and-f-35c-plans-are-detailed-for-the-first-time/.
3. https://www.bbc.com/news/uk-politics-18008171.